Praise for

'Bold and uncomprom ... work is a requiem for Lloyd's beloved husband and a testimony to her own survival. It is valiant, compelling writing . . . candid, gritty, raw.' THE AGE

'This book is both profound and universal. It is a truly remarkable piece of writing, which should be read by everyone who wants to understand the mysteries of love and death.'
THE SYDNEY MORNING HERALD

'Lloyd's honesty and simple writing style is deeply compelling.'
MARIE CLAIRE

'a nuanced story of love and loss . . . both uplifting and harrowing'
THE SUN-HERALD

'Lloyd contours grief and all the unexpected ways in which a death can change a life.' THE SUNDAY MAIL

'The ending of Lloyd's book is no surprise, but her joy in the simple, everyday pleasures of a loving relationship, however long it lasts, gives pause for thought.' THE COURIER-MAIL

'a beautiful memoir . . . Lloyd's thoughts on life without her soul mate . . . leave you feeling happy that there could be such love in the world.' AUSTRALIAN BOOKSELLER & PUBLISHER

'This book's power lies in its gentle reminder that . . . at the end of your days to have loved and be loved is the greatest achievement of all.' GOOD READING

Virginia Lloyd is a writer and consultant who lives in Sydney. She spent eighteen months in New York while writing *The Young Widow's Book of Home Improvement*. Her work has appeared in publications from *Vogue* to *Griffith Review*, and she is currently writing her next book.

www.virginialloyd.com
www.youngwidowsbook.com

The
Young
Widow's Book of
Home Improvement

Virginia Lloyd

UQP

First published 2008 by University of Queensland Press
PO Box 6042, St Lucia, Queensland 4067 Australia

This edition published 2009

www.uqp.com.au

Text design by Sandy Cull, gogoGingko, and Christabella Designs
Typesetting by Pauline Haas, Bluerinse Setting
Printed in Australia by McPherson's Printing Group
Author photograph by Peter McCarthy
Illustration courtesy iStockphoto

Cataloguing-in-publication Data
National Library of Australia

Lloyd, Virginia
The young widow's book of home improvement
ISBN 978 0 7022 3737 9 (pbk)
Lloyd, Virginia – Biography. Widows – Biography. Grief
– Psychological aspects. Bereavement – Psychological
aspects. Widowhood – Psychological aspects. Dwellings
– Remodelling – Psychological aspects.
155.937092

The names of a few secondary characters have been changed.

University of Queensland Press uses papers that are natural, renewable and recyclable
products made from wood grown in sustainable forests. The logging and manufacturing
processes conform to the environmental regulations of the country of origin.

Contents

Memory

NATALIA GINZBURG

Men come and go through the city's streets.
They buy food and newspapers, they have their jobs to do.
They have rosy faces, rich full lips.
You lifted the sheet to look at his face,
You leaned down to kiss him in the same old way.
But it was the last time. It was the same face,
Just a little more tired. And the suit was the same.
And the shoes were the same. And the hands were those
That would break the bread and pour the wine.
Today, with the time moved on, you still lift the sheet
To see his face for the last time.
If you walk along the street, nobody is beside you.
If you are afraid, nobody takes your hand.
And it isn't your street, it isn't your city.
It isn't your city which is all lit up: the city all lit up belongs to others,
To the men who come and go buying food and newspapers.
You can look out for a while from the quiet window
And look in silence at the garden in the dark.
Then when you cried there was his calming voice.
Then when you laughed there was his obliging smile.
But the gate that would be opened at night will be shut forever;
And your youth is gone, the fire is out, the house is empty.

Part One

Rising Damp

1

'Would it be all right with ye if I came back and took a photo of this wall, here, y'know, for me website?' asked Jim, the Irish anti-damp expert who had come to assess the damage to my home.

I was flattered, picturing a dazzling 'before' and 'after' comparative case study, until I realised what he meant. 'I haven't seen it as bad as this in a long time,' Jim continued softly, gesturing at either side of the fireplace in the living room. 'Any reason ye left it for so long?'

Despite Jim's best efforts to keep his tone curious but disinterested, I had seen his eyes widen in disbelief as he took in the detailed plasterwork around the fireplace in our living room crumbling to the floor, the rotted timber in every windowsill, and the billowing air pockets where excess moisture had literally forced the paint away from the walls with a destructive flourish.

What Jim really meant was, *How could you have let it get this bad?* I felt a bit sorry for Jim. He'd just been ambushed by a prospective client, and was trying not to look shocked at the damage that years of untreated rising damp had perpetrated on the interior and exterior walls of this grand old Victorian house in inner-western Sydney. He could probably earn quite a bit on this job, I could see him thinking, due to the sheer number of walls affected. So he needed to frame his question with care. He must avoid seeming judgemental: after all, rising damp was his stated field of expertise, and the very problem I had called him in to evaluate.

My husband, John, and I could hardly *ignore* some of the more visible evidence of our home's decay. We knew there was a damp problem to which houses like ours — semi-detached, double-brick, and built in the late nineteenth century — were particularly susceptible. The decaying mouldings and peeling paint were tangible signs of our neglect. There was no denying the problem when we could clearly see, month after month, the ten-year-old paint blistering and the rendered surface of the walls in our living room crumbling into piles of the finest dust in front of our eyes. They looked like those delicate mounds of sifted flour in the mixing bowl before you add the egg. But we did nothing. In confessing our domestic mismanagement, I can say only in our defence that, at the time, we had a bigger problem than the rising damp. It was my forty-seven-year-old husband. He was dying.

As Jim took me on a guided tour of the structural damage to my home caused by the untreated damp problem, the scale of work required to address it became apparent. Inside the house the damage was much more pronounced than it was on the outside. Almost every internal wall was home to mould spores: the tiny black dots clustered in ones and twos like tumours in the least damp rooms, but fanned out across the ceiling of the laundry and bathroom like an invading army. For us the mould had been a noticeable but benign presence: asthma was one condition that John did not have to contend with, and in my family it was my younger brother, my only sibling, who inherited the asthmatic gene.

Until this moment I had freely admired the black patches of varied shape and size that flared out from every nail in our elderly wooden floorboards. Visitors had often remarked on the unusual patterns as an attractive feature of our home's interior décor. Jim explained that the patches were the result of the wet air trapped underneath the boards meeting the metal nails. He frowned at the black patches as he talked, which suggested his displeasure at their existence. Their varied patterns indicated *rust*. I should have been horrified at the revelation of the patterns' true genealogy, but my heart went out to these blackened sheep. Perhaps it was my perspective, dampened by grief, but on any given day I saw in those rust patches either a young girl or an old woman. At thirty-four I certainly felt old, very old, and way too young, all at the same time.

So when Jim asked why I had left it so long to get some professional help, he knew exactly how much time it would have taken for the damp — and the damage — to get to the serious level ours had attained. His question was reasonable. Logical. But the real question I struggled to get my mind around, as I shifted weight from one foot to the other, was how to answer it. I had hoped, given he was Irish, that Jim would have some intuition about why I had asked him to quote on this job for me. My husband was Irish too; a North Londoner born and bred, perhaps, but raised by parents from north-western Ireland's County Mayo and County Sligo.

Although John had become an Australian citizen as soon as he was eligible, on our honeymoon he had proudly brandished his red Irish passport at every port of entry to a new country. In the split second before answering I rehearsed possible responses in my head.

It's funny, you know, Jim, mostly we didn't notice it. But I couldn't say that because now he had pointed out the extensive damage it seemed impossible that we didn't notice it. But we simply didn't have time, especially in our last six months together, when we were busy with the relentless demands of John's regime of medication and palliative care. *When we began to notice the damage, we chose to ignore it, because it wasn't a priority.* There was no way I could say that to a professional for whom addressing rising damp was his life's work. *We were too busy trying to stave off my husband's death from an excruciatingly painful form of secondary bone cancer.* Ah, there's the reason. The umbrella reason that contained all possible other reasons. But it was the one response I was not prepared to give him.

The risks of an honest answer were multiple. Jim might get that look on his face — a fumbling mess of confusion, awkwardness, pity — and I'd feel compelled to say something glib to make him feel less uncomfortable with this new and unexpected knowledge of his client. Or Jim might be one of those 'oh well, they say time heals all wounds' types; or worse, suspect that I might be playing the sympathy card in order to elicit a discounted quote for the work. On the other hand, Jim might think it's a great chance to offer a high quote for the job and count on the fact that I'm in no state of mind to sort through numerous quotes. (In which case he would have been absolutely correct.)

'Oh, for various reasons my husband and I didn't get around to it,' I said, casually. It was a version of the truth.

'Fair enough,' said Jim, keeping judgement to himself. He sat down on the sofa to write up the quote. As far as he was concerned, my husband was at work and I would discuss the numbers with him when he got home.

2

The doorbell rang for the third time that morning. 'If that's another bunch of flowers I am going to scream,' I yelled to my sister-in-law from the bathtub as she made her way through my house to open the front door. Sheila had dropped everything, including her two young children, to race from Dublin to Sydney to see John one last time. She had heard the unmistakable deathly rasp of his voice during their last phone call, when John was in the hospital. Having nursed their mother through the late stages of stomach cancer five years earlier, she recognised immediately John's difficulty in forming words, in breathing, and his battle-weariness after so many years of valiant struggle. In the end she missed her older brother by less than twenty-four hours. She was somewhere in the air over England at the time, on her way to Heathrow for her connecting flight to Sydney.

Sheila was the middle child and only girl of three evenly spaced, even-tempered children, born four years apart. She and John had won numerous trophies together as adolescents in ballroom dancing competitions. When John's attention turned to football, Sheila's competitive focus became fencing. She ended up at the World Championships. Sheila had the heart of a lion inside the wiry pocket-sized frame of a ballet dancer. At Heathrow she learned from our mutual friend Maria that her older brother was dead.

I had sent Maria a text message from the hospital, so she could race to the airport to save Sheila the long flight. She telephoned from Heathrow, to ask if it would be all right if she continued her journey to Sydney to help me with the arrangements. Too stunned to say otherwise, I agreed. I had no idea what constituted *arrangements*. When she arrived the next morning, I was overwhelmed with the relief of being able to collapse, weeping, in the arms of someone else who loved John. Someone else whom John had loved.

I settled back into my bath and caressed the water around me, trying to return to the state of morbid stillness I had been approximating for the past ten minutes. I was trying to remain submerged for as long as it was humanly possible. Longer would have been preferable.

The day John died a single deep purple rose had bloomed in our front garden. In the three days since then there had been many strangers at my door holding bouquets of flowers. The news of his death was contagious; it spread quickly and produced unexpected side-effects. 'Are you Virginia?' one delivery man asked me. When I nodded dumbly, he thrust a gorgeous explosion of colour into my hands. 'These are for you,' he grinned. 'Congratulations!'

It was small comfort to know he hadn't read the card attached.

Thinking of you at this sad time.

Sheila dutifully carried in the latest arrangement, but we had already run out of vases. As I lay immersed to my chin, trying to ignore the intrusive, persistent sound of my own breathing, I could hear her opening and closing cupboards in an effort to find a receptacle to house the fresh buds, more young flowers whose short lives were claimed to mark another life cut down in its prime. The exquisite bouquets kept arriving over those first ten days, so we were forced to improvise. Soon arrangements tilted in the tall pot I used to cook spaghetti. Others jostled for position in the blue bucket into which John had vomited his half-digested ice cream. That had only been two weeks ago. Already it felt like a lifetime.

From my reclining position I looked up at the ceiling of our bathroom and saw the undeniable evidence of decay. In some places the paint was blistering, full of what I imagined to be pockets of air; in others it was peeling away in strips. Had the ceiling been this bad when I moved in two years ago? Perhaps it was just that until this week I'd had no time to notice its decrepitude. Neither had I previously observed the black dots clustered near the blistering paint.

Everything fights to survive, I thought. Even mould.

The bathroom ceiling was a microcosm of the rising damp problem that pervaded the entire house. Moisture, which arrived from outside in the usual ways — rain, storm water, poorly draining soil — had become trapped between the bricks, between the ground and the floor, and within the walls themselves. The moisture decided to stay in the notoriously porous and hospitable surface of the house's sandstone foundations. But there were no air vents to let fresh air in, to dry out the resident water. When the foundations had absorbed as much moisture as they possibly could, the excess water eventually defied gravity and moved upwards by capillary action. As it rose up our walls, the evaporating water pulled salts and minerals towards the surface of the stone and brickwork. And by this simple process, invisible to the naked eye, complex and visible havoc — rotting plaster, blistering and peeling paint — was wreaked.

Water surrounded me. After a year of drought conditions in most parts of Australia, October 2004 was exceedingly wet. A severe downpour had finally toppled the dilapidated fence that marked the boundary between the back of our house and the parking area for the apartment block next door. The rain respected neither suburban borders nor our privacy. If the water saw an entry point to our house, it invited itself in. During the downpour I discovered the extent of the party: the roof of the deck that extended from the house to the garden, where John and I had enjoyed so many hours and meals together, was full of holes; while inside, the v-shaped ceiling in the hallway at the back half of the house dripped from its lowest point in imitation of the meeting place, directly above it, of the two gutters on the roof. Yet another plastic container had to be found to collect the drops that fell with soft precision to the floorboards. Despite its sudden and multifarious appearance, I could control this water. I could *see* it, lay out my palm and collect the drops as they fell inside the house. I even knew when to expect it, like the annual visit from a distant relative. The deeper, more insidious problem relating to water was the water that I could not directly see, but which had nevertheless been making its presence felt.

For all its quiet grandeur, the house was showing its age. In the early 1890s two Scottish brothers subdivided a parcel of land on the gently sloping hill where they kept pigs and built two houses with an adjoining wall down the middle. The piggery is long gone, but the houses, identical in their layout but symmetrically opposed, remain. Mine is one of them. In real-estate speak I live in what's known as a double-fronted semi-detached home. To the untrained eye it looks like any other construction of the Victorian era — solid, indestructible — although in this case twice as wide as the standard semi.

The burnt-butter colour adorning the exterior of the house was unflattering and dated, a favourite old suit that no longer fit the body for which it had been originally tailored. If you looked more closely, you could see that the paint was peeling off the walls — not in great swaths, like bark from a eucalyptus tree, but more like the straggly bits of cuticle that pop up suddenly around your fingernails. The paint fell off with more urgency in certain places — around the windowsills, anywhere close to drainpipes, or near to the ground — and, most dramatically, all the way across the imposing front of our house and the decorative tiles that covered the layer of bricks where the wall met the front porch, creating a perverse additional border around the edges of the tiles. What was revealed after the dirty pale-yellow paint had peeled off was some unappealing dark grey cement that felt icy cold to the touch. The reason it was so cold was that it was full of water. The bits of paint peel lay about in fragments until the strong wind that liked to gust down our street swept them away, or those irregular occasions when I remembered to gather them up with a broom.

The house clearly needed our attention, but John and I needed each other more. We were in no doubt about what needed to be done. Or in what order those tasks needed doing. Before anything else, we had to fix the rising damp. Second, render the affected walls. Third, paint the house inside and out. *We*. It was as simple, and as impossible, as that.

During our discussions about the state of our home, one fact remained understood but unspoken: that I would have to tackle the renovation effort alone from start to finish. Home improvement would be my sole responsibility. Perhaps John took some comfort in knowing I would have something to keep me busy when he was no longer around. He had seen enough evidence of my tendency towards chronic organisation to feel confident about my ability to get the necessary jobs done. Even better, he loved me in spite of it. But neither of us ever imagined quite how pre-occupied I would become with my homework. Now there was nothing stopping me from attending to it. John was dead: I had all the time in the world.

The bouquets of flowers all died at the same time. They wilted, they drooped; the water turned cloudy. The rank odour of several dying bouquets was so overpowering it lingers in my memory. I preferred receiving cards, DVDs, and meals that could be frozen and eaten later. The flowers could wait. The time when I yearned to receive flowers was three, four, six months after John's death. That's when his absence was devastatingly real to me, and made more so by the fact that no one thinks to send flowers then. That was the acrid moment when I realised that everyone else had, in one way or another, moved on with their lives.

Now, with the flowers newly dead like my husband, all I could think of to do was to lie completely still, in my increasingly long and increasingly late-night baths, and let the music I chose to accompany me express fractions of my emotions: anguish, inertia, despair, isolation, longing, consternation, grief, heartbreak, loss, loneliness, sorrow, yearning. Usually my musical selection included the piano — my first love — and was mostly instrumental music of the past few decades. For want of a better word, a lot of this music is called *jazz*, but it's often inadequate for the descriptive task. My head and my heart have always found equal refuge in its combination of improvisation and harmonic structure. The music expresses freedom and constraint simultaneously; the freedom to improvise is in fact only created *through* the structures of melody and harmony that provide choices for the improvisation. A jazz musician cannot improvise without the melody and a harmonic structure from which to take flight. Well, technically it is possible, but I cannot listen to the results without wanting to cut off my ears. My favourite recordings transport me with the simultaneous creativity of the individual musicians and the group's interdependence in performance. Often I needed to hear my favourite pianists, Bill Evans, Mike Nock, Brad Mehldau. Sometimes it was a saxophonist's or a trumpet player's band. I love the quiet intensity of instrumental music from Scandinavia and Poland, and listened obsessively to Bobo Stenson and Thomas Stanko. As the water lapped around me, my heart was temporarily suspended in the dissonant beauty of the complex chords that wafted through the house.

One jazz aficionado friend of mine calls some of this stuff 'music to slit your wrists by', so I probably should have been more careful. There have been many times since John died when I thought about suicide, particularly in the first six months. But I did not want to kill myself. I just yearned desperately not to be alive. I longed to be without consciousness, without sensation, without feeling. I would have given anything even to swap places with John, so he could come back. The world would be a better place with him in it rather than me, I thought, so I would agree to an exchange . . . if I could just find out how to arrange it. Living, *breathing*, was so hard. I had never been so conscious before of my own heartbeat, regular as clockwork. The phrase 'rude health' took on fresh significance because my own good health felt like an unwanted intrusion. It felt disrespectful to John for me not to be experiencing any physical complaints.

Even during the moments I thought like this I recognised the passivity of my intense desire to be not-alive. I would entertain brief daydreams in which I became not-alive through a variety of third-party events. For example, by being run over by a bus on a major thoroughfare in broad daylight, or by one of those oversize four-wheel drives careering down my street at dusk; alternatively, by falling through the air as the balcony I stood on gave way through faulty construction. My favourite fantasy was being diagnosed with a massive brain tumour or other acute condition and having days to live. Being able to defiantly, nobly refuse treatment in order to hurry things along. Somehow I felt that I needed a couple of days just to finalise things before I could see John again. Whatever those things might have been.

3

When I first met John I was thirty-two years old, living by myself in Sydney's inner-western suburbs, and saving up for a deposit on an apartment. A refugee from the book publishing industry where I had worked as a copy-editor, I had fled to the comparatively dull but well-paid country of the corporate world, where I managed the client publishing activities of a major law firm. It turned out that the legal services industry valued the same diplomatic and editorial skills I had used working with writers at almost twice the price of my former employer.

After having shared apartments, eaten Thai take-away and gratefully used other people's furniture for so long, living alone was a revelation. Renting my own apartment gave me the opportunity to begin to shape my adult life in concrete and more intangible ways. I bought furniture I actually liked. I played my electronic keyboard when I felt like it. I caught up on films I'd always meant to see at the cinema or was too embarrassed to rent in front of flatmates. I taught myself to cook and invited friends over for dinner. This one-bedroom sanctuary was the still point of my moving world. Most of the time I wasn't lonely — there were always too many books to read, friends to see, exceptional and obscure jazz musicians to go and listen to at the club around the corner from where I lived — but I did spend a lot of time alone.

Throughout my twenties I had lived from day to day, saving up for or paying off trips to New York. The city had fascinated me since I was a teenager, when I first began paying closer attention to my father's jazz collection and watching Woody Allen films. (The good ones.) While still a postgraduate student in the English Literature department of the University of Sydney, before taking my first tentative steps in the world of book publishing, I had even entered the annual green card lottery for the chance of living and working in the USA.

I had been single for more than two years — for so long, in fact, that I no longer thought of myself in those terms. My previous significant relationship had been an exhilarating joyride that turned gradually into a slow-motion collision, my thirtieth birthday the appropriately ceremonial occasion on which the ride had come to a crashing stop. That birthday seems to be a crossroads for many women. As the first-born child and only daughter in a socially and politically conservative household, I had learned over the years to keep my feelings mostly to myself. Dissent was dangerous, so distance became my specialty. I gradually internalised any hint of conflict or distress to the extent that I myself was barely aware of feeling any. It was safer, if exhausting, just to keep smiling.

So the end of this relationship wasn't entirely my boyfriend's fault. He had been consistently himself from the moment I met him. His wanton disregard for what other people thought or felt was one of the many things I admired, even envied, about him.

He had no idea I was unhappy and, until right before I yanked the plug, neither did I. Keeping everyone else happy had been the easier course of action for a textbook good-girl.

With triangular predictability, a third party entered my drama a few months prior to my fateful thirtieth birthday. I would call Upstage Left my *deus ex machina*, except that he was all too human. He was but the latest in a line of older men who had admired me fervently at arm's length. Upstage Left said things like, 'Why hasn't he asked you to marry him?' and 'Doesn't he want to have children with you? You would be such a wonderful mother'. These were questions I did not want to hear. They were already loud enough in my head, where they had been gathering volume for months.

Ever since I've been able to notice, I have been one of those women who attract ardent older admirers. This is not something I am proud of. I would have preferred to date men my own age, but they never dared ask me out. Most often my admirers were at least ten years my senior, and aside from the generic physiological attributes of a pale-skinned brunette with an hourglass figure, I'm not sure what it was about me in particular that attracted them. I presented a polished, charming and articulate exterior, a woman who loved watching cricket and reading books (if not in equal measure), and who could talk about most subjects with most people. I had a masters degree in the sort of banter that passes for conversation in inner-city social circles. My handbag and shoes generally matched. Maybe it was more about what attracted me to them: these platonic friendships gave me the opportunity of interesting conversation and the illusion of intimacy at a safe distance. I was secure on a pedestal of my own making.

Upstage Left was looking to exit the drama of his own loveless marriage, and his stage directions indicated I was the answer to his prayers. I couldn't really understand why he was sending gifts and tapes and poems to my office and wanting to see me when he knew I was in a relationship, or why I turned up to meet him for coffee or a glass of wine even though I was sure I loved my boyfriend.

Incredibly naive, yes, but I was dim to the seriousness of his intentions, and even less aware of my own motives, for much longer than I should have been. Even now I am ashamed to admit that I let him imagine some utopian future in which he and I might happily co-exist. At one point I even introduced my boyfriend to my admirer at an exhibition, knowing in advance that we would run into each other. Somehow I thought that we could all become friends, have dinner together, see films. At that point I was not only in denial, but operating under the assumption that his wife knew I existed. My boyfriend understood the situation much more simply. After the exhibition, in his usual blunt and unsentimental fashion he said, 'This guy wants to fuck your brains out. Can't you see that? Listen, if you want to have an affair with him, go ahead, just make sure you come back to me.'

~

At the beach one day soon afterwards, I pointed to a young father helping his toddler build a sandcastle. 'Can you see yourself doing that?' I asked my boyfriend.

He looked up and saw what I was pointing at. 'No, not really,' he said, and went back to reading his book. Evidently that was the end of the conversation. Looking at father and son working together in the sand, I thought how easily their castle could be obliterated by a single unexpected wave. What else was there for me to say to my boyfriend? I didn't know why I even asked the question. I hated myself for dwelling for days on his curt response, for focusing on children. I didn't particularly want children, and castigated myself for such socially conservative thinking. Part of the reason I was with this man, I reminded myself, was that he was so unlike everyone else; he had shaken me out of the intellectual cloak I had shrouded myself in for so many years.

It soon dawned on me that whether or not I wanted to have children was beside the point. There was no safety net to our trapeze act. If I *did* eventually want to have a child, I realised with a shock, I didn't want to have a child with him. I was a long way up to recognise that in this relationship I was alone with a long way to fall, whether by myself or with some imaginary child in tow. This seems now like such a small shift in my perspective, but at the time it was momentous. That was the day I began to dismantle the scaffold on which my relationship had been so precariously built.

~

Within a few weeks both men had exited my stage, and I was once again alone upon it — relieved to be free of them both, but carrying the burden of responsibility for the failed relationship squarely on my own two shoulders. There was a queasy familiarity to the knot in my stomach. I was determined to get to the bottom of why I was feeling so wretched and so much a failure, why I could not concentrate or stop crying, why the books and music that usually sustained me held no appeal. Suddenly it was critical that I understand why there were so many fleeting echoes of relationships past in my isolated present.

Referral in hand, I went to see a psychotherapist. Our regular sessions over a period of months were the best investment I could ever have made. I had no idea how far removed from everyone else I was. Even in their midst. The transformation from closed to open was gradual, but it was permanent. These days I am so evangelical that I consider the therapeutic process my road to Damascus. Ironically, many people who had known me for a long time might not have noticed any particular change in me over the years — the sort of psychological revolution I experienced has mostly been invisible, and my interior state now broadly matches the surface I had long presented to the world — but I know I am profoundly and permanently changed. I know it because my relationships with my family and closest friends are richer, more intimate; I know it because this change in me led to greater confidence and success in my professional life; and I know it because, when the time finally came, it allowed me to recognise John as the man I'd been looking for.

⁓

'Why in the world would you want to go to *America*?' John asked incredulously when we finally met. I had just told him of my plan to move to New York within the next twelve months: on my fourth attempt I had won a green card in the annual lottery. John couldn't understand why anyone would want to leave Sydney. Certainly not to live in the United States.

I had started getting to know John long before I ever met him in person. His name often came up in conversation whenever I was at my friends Paul and Anne's place for dinner. John and Paul used to play on the same local soccer team, but these days they watched rather than played sport together. John was such a regular topic of conversation that if my friends didn't offer any information about how he was doing, I would always ask. I knew that their friend of many years had been battling some form of cancer, and that at some point his Australian-born wife, with whom he had moved to Sydney six years earlier, had left him. That was the sum total of my knowledge of John. Height, weight, job, hair colour, musical taste, sense of humour: of these things I knew nothing. Without knowing any details of the nature or extent of his illness, I felt instinctive empathy for someone struggling alone with cancer. Ignorant of the multitudes and vicissitudes of the complex of diseases within that broad category, I assumed that, whatever sort of cancer John had, he was receiving the proper treatment and would look forward to eventual recovery and a future of his own making.

John had fallen in love with Sydney almost immediately. After a long and steady career in London in the IT department of Marks & Spencer, he quickly found work as a systems engineer in a small technology start-up that was later bought out by a large telecommunications company. When I met him, John enjoyed his job only slightly less than the uninterrupted view of the harbour from his office. He got a thrill every morning as he drove underneath the southern pylon of the Sydney Harbour Bridge on his way to work, and nothing gave him greater pleasure than sending his friends in cold dank London photographs full of sunshine and open spaces. He was always hosting one or another friend who had made the long journey to discover the city for themselves.

'New York is not America,' I said, and not for the last time. 'It's such an exciting city, full of energy, creativity. I have always felt so inspired by spending time there absorbing the art, the music, the museums and the theatre —'

'Don't you enjoy those things here?' he said, looking intently at me. I liked his curiosity, and that he wasn't going to easily let me off the hook. He wasn't being defensive about his own feelings about Sydney; he genuinely wanted to understand my motivations.

'Yes,' I said, 'but I've just always wanted to live and work there for a while. For me New York is the epicentre of all those things.'

John smiled, his brown curly hair nodding with him. 'I know what you mean. I used to think London was the centre of the universe,' he said, 'but then I came to Sydney and discovered that there could be another one. This place is the centre of the world for me now.'

~

'That's quite a tan you've got,' I said to John at our next meeting, a dinner party at Paul and Anne's several months later. 'Have you been away somewhere?'

'No holiday to report, I'm afraid, just a side-effect of the chemo I've been having,' he said brightly, and stretched across the table to top up my wine glass. 'How are your travel plans coming along?'

'Oh, um, they're fine,' I said, trying to act as if I hadn't just exposed my foot-in-mouth disease for everyone at the dinner table to see. It intrigued me that John remembered so many details of our previous meeting. I described a few recent adventures in obtaining the requisite documentation — a criminal record check, a chest x-ray, a tetanus injection, fingerprints. But deep down I felt ambivalent about the prospect of leaving Sydney. *Be careful what you wish for*, a clairvoyant had once told me. It had taken years to understand what she meant. I didn't have a clue what I'd do when I got to New York, but at least my paperwork would be exemplary.

The room's dim lighting hid my blush. I felt like such an idiot for confusing the effects of chemotherapy and sunshine, but instinctively also knew there was no need for me to feel that way. While the rest of us were trying our best not to say the wrong thing, John was disarmingly pragmatic and straightforward about his illness.

A fanatical traveller, John was about to jet off to South Korea to take in a few matches at the 2002 World Cup, soccer's four-yearly championship. He had seen much of Europe by virtue of having lived in London for so many years. Driving around Ireland on a motorbike as a young man, he had gained a prosthetic knuckle in the middle finger of his right hand as a memento of the time he came off the bike on a long stretch of one of its quiet country roads. With his brother, David, and a few mates he had toured England's canals in a houseboat, and had the snapshots of their debauched antics to prove it. Now John wanted to take advantage of the hospitality of an old friend who was working in Seoul, who also had access to semi-final tickets. The year before that he had spent time in Beijing with a painter friend who had an artist's residency there. He was planning a trip to the America's Cup in Auckland in February. I was impressed: this was a man who wasted no time.

I quickly understood that, while cancer was undeniably part of John's life, it did not define him. Rather, it provided the context in which he went about living his life. He considered himself a fighter constantly battling an invisible opponent. Sometimes he'd literally call it 'the enemy' or 'that bastard Cancer'. The subject line of his occasional emails to friends on the topic of his treatment was always the same: 'Cancer Boy Update'.

Looking at John's thick brown hair across the dinner table, I realised his very short cropped style was due not to a severe haircut but to natural regrowth after chemotherapy. It seemed less curly than I remembered it before the treatment. I never asked him directly about it. Like most people, I suppose, I was nervous of broaching such a personal subject with someone whom I knew but couldn't quite describe as a friend. So we talked about food and books and travel and politics and wine instead. Without knowing it, my general curiosity about people was turning into a much deeper and enduring fascination with this one man.

I could tell John liked me, and it made me nervous. Other than his illness I couldn't figure out what was wrong with him. With my procession of older admirers, I had always been clear about why each was unsuitable. And while John was older than me — I wasn't sure exactly how much older; he had such boyish exuberance he seemed much younger than the forty-something years I attributed to him — there wasn't a hint of the passive arms-length admiration I had come to be able to spot a mile away. John and I chatted as easily as if we'd known each other for years. Physically we were almost exactly the same height. He offered no pedestal for me to stand on, and to my delight I realised I needed none. I was standing firmly on solid earth, enjoying the view from ground level.

We usually drank a lot of wine at Paul and Anne's. One night after a couple of glasses of McLaren Vale's finest I related a novel invention I had heard about at work during the week. A colleague had told me about a couple he knew who were so earnest about collecting wine that they owned a computerised tracking system, which told them not only where every bottle of wine was stored in their cellar, but also the right time to drink each one. Vintage, terroir, tasting notes — you name it, this couple relied on their computer to tell them what to drink and when. The only thing it didn't do was prepare the meal to match the ripest bottle.

Telling this story, my astonishment at their technical sophistication mixed with tipsy admiration of their passion for wine. After holding forth for a minute or so, I became aware of some smirking going on across the dinner table. After a short symphony of raised eyebrows, discreet coughs and knowing looks from our mutual friends, John finally confessed that he, too, owned a software program that he relied on to manage his cellar. His love of technology's practical applications was not limited to his job.

I giggled at John's embarrassment, and was relieved to see that he could also laugh at himself. 'Well maybe one of these days I'll get an invitation to see this cellar of yours,' I teased. The words flew out of my mouth before I realised what they meant: not only did I like this man, but I wasn't scared of him. I was flirting because I trusted him. I hadn't felt those things together before.

John later claimed it was this gentle challenge that gave him hope I might be interested in more than just talking to him around the dinner party table. He promptly invited me to his place for a barbecue a few nights later to help farewell some friends from London who were visiting him at the time.

~

As it turned out, I lived only ten minutes' walk away from John's house. It had taken much less time to get there than it had to decide what I should wear. When I turned up at the address John had given me, the street was dark but the house was full of light. The front gate opened with a welcoming squeak.

Often we need retrospect to see the narrative of our life unfolding, marked by those occasional events that move our own plot forward. But at this barbecue, I could feel something momentous happening. During the course of the evening I was unable to take my eyes off John. Every time he moved, my eyes moved with him. I remember feeling as though a curtain made of the finest material, transparent and perhaps invisible to this moment, was being lifted from my eyes, and I was seeing John in full for the very first time. I was struck by how lovely he was, how kind; how generous and thoughtful to his friends. I saw how much they loved him. I remembered how disappointed I'd been to turn up at our friends' home for dinner only recently to discover that John wouldn't be joining us that night.

How he makes me laugh, I thought. I'm so at ease around him. *But we're just friends.* John set up a series of wine glasses at the table to show me the difference when the same wine is tasted from differently shaped glasses. I wondered if he was this attentive to all his guests. His love of breaking into a scarily accurate Cockney accent had to now obscured his beautiful speaking voice, which suddenly enchanted me. *But I'm moving to New York next year.* All the paperwork is in motion. I've had my fingerprints taken, my police record checked, tetanus shots, even a cursory medical check by a doctor approved by the US Department of Immigration who squeezed my breasts like he was tooting a bicycle horn during a cursory check for lumps. These dubious pleasures have so far cost me hundreds of dollars. *But I haven't thought about John like that before.* Having feelings for John was not part of my plan. I had scoffed at those friends who suggested I would meet someone just as I was leaving for New York. 'It's always when it happens,' they all said. *But he's so handsome. I never noticed how blue his eyes are. He's smiling at me with gentleness and cheek in equal measure.* It was so refreshing to meet a man who was not trying to prove anything to anyone. One more week of chemotherapy, he says, then it's over. He looks so well. So comfortable in his own skin. I don't know how old he is, but he's too young to be really sick. *I don't care how old he is.*

At the end of the barbecue, I kissed John on the cheek and pulled him closer for a hug. I was trying to find a moment to talk with him privately but the Greek chorus of friends surrounded us. So I suggested he and I meet for coffee at the end of the week, when his chemotherapy was finished. To my relief he agreed. Aromatherapy, psychotherapy, chemotherapy; it's no big deal, I thought. People have chemotherapy all the time. He's getting treatment, so he's getting better. That's what happens.

~

Walking along Castlereagh Street the next day, my head full of thoughts about John, I rang my mother. These days she waited for me to ask for her opinion. I needed it. Like true north, I could rely on her point of view to be completely straight, even if I didn't always like the direction in which it pointed.

'I've met someone I like,' I said casually.

'That's good,' she replied, as if she heard me say words to this effect every week. 'What's he like?'

'He's really . . . nice,' I said. 'Funny, interesting. A friend of Paul and Anne's. He's —' I stopped. I didn't know how to put it. 'But he's got cancer.'

'Oh no, really? How bad is it?' she asked.

'I'm not sure. The thing is, he looks really well. I really like him.'

'Well there aren't many good ones around,' Mum said. 'You know what you're doing.'

~

One coffee turned into a five-hour lunch, during which we hardly stopped talking to eat and I could not wait to kiss him — or for him to kiss me — it didn't matter which. I had found what I had been looking for, much closer to home than I'd dreamed possible. New York suddenly seemed a very long way away. But to my chagrin John didn't even try to hold my hand. A few days later, as he walked me home from another dinner at our friends' place, our hands suddenly and magically intertwined. Inside my apartment, I closed the door. It was dark except for the moonlight that shone through the large windows. At last, it was just the two of us, face to face.

'I hope you're going to kiss me,' I said.

4

My unconscious philosophy — organise or perish — was in operation within hours of John's death.

On the very day my parents collected me from the hospital, I organised. I made phone calls. To my closest friends. To my assistant at work. 'Oh, Virginia,' I heard her gasp, 'I'm so sorry.' The wave started building in the pit of my stomach as she started to cry so I hung up quickly.

I sat down at the computer and composed this message announcing John's death to his friends and colleagues, to all who knew him and cared about us. It was twelve hours since he had died.

My wonderful, beautiful husband John died peacefully in my arms just before two o'clock this morning. As many of you know he fought a rare tumour for more than seven years with his unique blend of determination, grace and humour. He endured more pain than anyone should ever have to experience, but right up to the last he was still very much the man we know and love, enjoying life to the full as much as was possible under the circumstances. About three weeks ago we knew things had changed when he was no longer interested in food, not even in his beloved wine, and he suddenly lost a lot of weight. After that point he deteriorated rapidly and was admitted to hospital last Saturday afternoon. Last night he was comfortable and free from pain when he passed away slowly with me by his side.

Those of you who know us both know how much we loved each other and we felt so lucky to have been able to spend even this short period of time together.

Two days ago John gave me a message to send to his friends. He wanted you to know that he was very happy and considered himself a fortunate man.

'If you have half as much of a wonderful time that I've enjoyed on this planet, you will be very lucky fellows indeed. I thank you all for your deep friendships and I have loved your friendships, which have given me joy, strength, but most of all, plenty of the craic. If I was with you now I'd be standing here with a pint of the dark stuff, leaning against a bar somewhere around the world.'

The extreme trauma I was in makes remembering these things feel like they happened to someone else. I can see her now, sitting at the keyboard, putting words together. The computer was a safe place for her. Much safer than the bed or the sofa or the back deck. The desktop was an environment she could control, not like outside the house where the October wind howled and an unseasonable chill swept down the street and strangers didn't know her world had just collapsed. The sentences came easily. They sat side by side comfortably. There was no arguing about who should sit where. The words respected her need to get them out quickly. She was reporting from a war-zone. She was in shell-shock.

It wasn't until about a year later that I realised the most solemn news I had ever had to deliver was sent in Comic Sans Serif font. John loved it because he was always sending jokes to his friends and that font conveyed his cheeky sense of fun. I was appalled, but could do nothing. I wept — not out of shame; I just missed with a sting in my chest the ways in which he counter-balanced my intensity.

That first night, two close friends looked after me. They ordered pizza and made me eat a slice. I opened a special bottle from the cellar. Why not? I thought. *What would John do? What would John want me to do?* I drank the wine. What I remember most vividly of that first night is the sensation of sitting still. It was so unusual, so foreign to me, after such a long time of constantly being in motion. Of having so many things to do for John as his primary care-giver. The palpable absence of a reason not to sit still. And what that absence signified.

How I wished he were alive and I was the one who had died.

~⌒⌐

Night became dawn became afternoon became evening. Was it time for breakfast, or dinner? What time was it, exactly? These questions made no sense, as I couldn't register any change in the day. I was dimly aware that time was passing, but I had no relationship to it and its details did not affect me. There was an elasticity to time in those first days after John's death that is impossible to capture in the routines of daily life. We are usually slaves to time, always checking the clock, figuring how much we can fit into the next hour, leave to tomorrow, or plan for the weekend. And here I was, floating free of time, beyond its dominion.

A couple of days passed before I realised there was a discrepancy between the actual time and that shown on my bedside clock. It's so easy not to notice such things because your entire being is focused on survival; all non-essential matters are simply held at bay. But on the second or third morning of waking up alone, I switched on the radio — for something to do; I had no interest in world affairs, let alone local ones. I was surprised to hear the five o'clock news bulletin, but only because in my semi-conscious state I realised my digital clock was displaying a different time — a time that did not begin with a five. The difference, I realised after a few more groggy seconds, was much more than one or two minutes. My curiosity piqued, I slowly figured out the difference between the time stated on the clock, and the actual time. It was difficult because, even at my best, my brain is not wired for that sort of computing. My clock was exactly forty-seven minutes slow. Exactly one minute for every year of John's life. Since when does a digital clock lose that much time? Nothing made sense to me, so I decided not to think about the possibilities this discrepancy represented.

My copy of Stephen Hawking's *A Brief History of Time* sat unread on my bookshelf a decade after buying it. Now was definitely not the right time, in any sense.

I can't remember whether I ate anything. My parents, who stopped by daily, made me endless cups of tea. My old Sicilian neighbour Connie brought me a plate with a large boiled chicken leg on it. At least, that's what I think she said it was. She and her husband, Frank, had enjoyed coming over to our house occasionally to see John. We provided them with a captive audience for their own catalogue of physical complaints. I put the chicken on the kitchen island and forgot about it. Returning later for a cup of tea, I saw flies taking advantage of my lack of interest in the food. At night, I ate pasta stirred through with portions of Bolognese sauce I had cooked and frozen weeks earlier. One night I watched a comedy on DVD called *Something's Gotta Give*. I remember feeling awkward and confused by the sound of my own giggling.

I tried, but failed, to sleep. The room at the back of our house had the least light, so I tried resting on the mattress that had been lying on the floor in there since our last overseas visitor had slept on it. But it was the middle of October, and the light stole through the windows very early. Daylight Savings would come into effect soon. Light, day, hours of sunshine — these were the last things I needed. I wanted darkness, rest, oblivion.

In contrast to my physical exhaustion, one of my most un-settling memories from those first days was a feeling of incredible sexual energy. My body seemed to be at war with itself: I felt both physically spent and highly aroused. Even in my state of semi-consciousness I interpreted this surge in energy as primal — some kind of adrenalin-fuelled instinct, part of a 'fight or flight' response. On an intellectual and emotional level the sensation was disturbing to me; but somehow on a physical, instinctual level it made sense. Rather, it made sense to my body in a way that made no sense to my mind. Getting rid of it was compulsive, like the need to sneeze. There was no pleasure in taking matters into my own hands. Instead, it felt like an unwanted obligation; the duty of allowing redundant steam to escape.

~ ॐ

In the meantime my father had made some calls regarding John's burial, and the office of Rookwood Cemetery had sent me a fax. It's strange to receive paperwork from a place calling itself 'The Necropolis', however accurate the Latin. 'Corpse City' doesn't have quite the same ring. My mind, hooked on wordplay, made a connection to the Acropolis of Athens. John's wanderlust had not abated, even after the cancer took away the use of his legs. I fantasised about receiving a postcard telling me he was in Ancient Greece, having a great time. *Wish you were here, Pumpkin. Forever yours, John.*

The fax included an information sheet and a map. Three 'plots' were marked with a cross on St John of God lawn, in the Catholic section of the cemetery. My task was to inspect the plots and select one to be John's final resting place. Which of the three had the happy ending, I wanted to ask. I decided not to ask the Necropolis. The cemetery office would not expect one of the Bereaved to ask whether the pun was intended.

Dad drove me out there. In the wake of the heavy rain the sun shone intensely. It was a blistering hot October day, one of those early harbingers of summer. I felt ridiculous walking around the manicured lawn neatly lined with headstones, navigating with a crude map marked with crosses. Of the three nominated plots, one was particularly appealing. Dappled sunlight filtered through the trees nearby. It felt different from the uniform rows of headstones quickly populating the lawn. Softer, somehow. I thought of John's pale freckled skin. I didn't want him to get sunburnt.

We got home and I rang the Necropolis. 'I've been out to … to the cemetery this morning,' I told the receptionist. 'I had a look at the available plots and I'd like number 237, please,' I said.

I'd like.

'Oh. I'm sorry, that one's taken,' she replied.

'What do you mean? You just faxed them to me yesterday,' I said.

'Yes, well, that one's taken now.' Her tone was brisk. She offered no explanation.

Thank goodness my father had suggested I select an alternative plot. The idea that someone else might die in the interim

— with whose family I would have to compete for poll position — hadn't occurred to me.

'Well . . . what about plot 255?'

'Um, that's gone too,' she said, consulting whatever records she kept close to hand. 'Yep — gone,' she repeated, in case I wasn't already familiar with the concept of absence.

I wondered why I had been offered three plots to select from in the first place if availability was so fleeting and unpredictable. An edge of desperation crept into my voice.

'Well, what — what have you got left?' I said, immediately transported several years into the past, into the world of hunting for an apartment. To her I was yet another anonymous voice, pleading for special consideration. Why did I feel like I was imposing on her? This morbid power trip of hers was the most untimely imposition on *me*. It was difficult to focus my attention on anything besides John's absence. Yet I was expected to process information, understand protocols, and make decisions. I was completely under this cemetery real-estate agent's spell.

She sensed the tremor in my voice and decided to soften her tone. 'Um . . . let me see. Plot 943 is nice. It's down the hill a little bit, on the far side of the lawn, beneath a big eucalyptus tree. That's still available.'

I took it sight-unseen. What else could I do? She had me over a barrel.

~

The next day I lingered in a local shop, a small boutique of exquisite things, because I wanted to tell the sales assistant that my husband had just passed away. I don't know why I was so determined to tell her. She was a complete stranger. I didn't quite understand how she could be carrying on her business as if nothing had happened. I finally bought a matching robe and slippers — partly because I knew I would be spending most of my time around the house; mainly because I felt I should buy something after dawdling in the shop for so long — and left without saying a word. I felt ashamed of myself for not speaking about John aloud to this woman, then pathetic for wanting to. My head was racing. Walking back home, I experienced an intense, almost overwhelming desire to drop my shopping bag, jump in a taxi and head straight to the airport. A toothbrush, my passport, credit card and a change of underwear: I could get a long way on so little. Maybe I could just disappear from my life. The prospect was enchanting, like I was casting a spell on myself. I could go anywhere. I could do anything. The absence of purpose was palpable, shocking. My lighthouse had disappeared. I was floating, but I didn't know where I was. Everything was dark.

5

Within three days of our first kiss, John presented me with my own set of keys, and by the end of that week we were more or less living under the same roof. After the confines of my small apartment, the house felt as large as the solar system, with its endless doors and rooms and soaring ceilings. I loved the heaviness of the front door as I pushed it open, and the way it rattled inside its frame when the wind blew it shut. I loved walking through the house, past our carpeted bedroom — dark from the heavy Chinese jasmine vines that hung across the front of the house, shielding the sun — into the living room, full of light from its exposed northern side. At the very back of the house was the kitchen, its marble-topped benches and double sink the height of luxury to a girl who had grown accustomed to a mini-fridge and no bench space whatsoever. I loved wandering through the house in the dark, getting to know my new home, the spongy feeling of the old floorboards beneath my bare feet. The ceilings seemed even higher in the dead of night. There was one wall in the living room that appeared as lonely as a blank canvas. It needed something on it — a painting, a photograph — but art could wait. There was history in this house, in the passage of years and eras to which it had been witness. There was the cumulative energy of the people who had lived and loved within its monumental walls. There was even a separate laundry. Finally,

I felt like a grown-up. Adults lived in houses. Adults had furniture they inherited or purchased complete, rather than cobbled together with an allen key.

~

'Ah, Dino. The one and only,' John said, as he pulled me up from the sofa and started twirling me around the living room. He was determined to teach me to dance. Over recent months the strains of 'That's Amore' had become almost as familiar to me as John's body.

'I've always been hopeless at this,' I said, embarrassed, as I stepped on his toes yet again. I longed to be a worthy dance partner for John, but felt like an elephant beside this man who was so elegant on his feet.

'You probably just never had a partner who knew what he was doing,' John said. Then he paused. 'You know, it would be a darn sight easier if you'd let me lead.' We burst out laughing.

As much as I delighted in dancing to Dean Martin, in discovering how easy it is for two people to make a bed, and in cooking dinner together at the end of our working days, my sudden transformation from living by myself to living with the man I had suddenly fallen in love with was not without growing pains. One day, a few weeks after I had moved in, John cornered me in the kitchen.

'What's the matter?' he said, sensing the agitation that had been building in me.

'I . . . don't know,' I said, not sure where to begin. Despite the therapy, it was still a difficult thing for me to feel safe on a conversational precipice.

'It's all right, Virginia,' he said, taking my hands in his. 'You can tell me anything. Talk to me.'

I had heard that before from someone I loved, and quickly been condemned for expressing how I felt. But I believed John.

'It's all happened so fast,' I blurted. 'You and me, moving in. So many changes . . . I think I just . . . need a bit of time. To get used to everything.'

'I understand. It's natural. It *has* happened quickly,' John said, his voice calm. He hadn't shrunk back in anger at my anxiety. Instead he had moved closer, and wrapped his arms around my waist. 'I guess I'm in more of a hurry because I've had a long time to get used to what's happened to me, and I don't know how much time I've got. But I don't want you to feel rushed. I want you to feel at home — here, with me, in this house. This is your home now, too.'

John and I were like two jigsaw pieces of different shapes that together made a snug fit. We bought tall narrow shelving to house John's punk and rock CDs and my jazz collection, which we combined and arranged alphabetically. John was curious about the obscure music I listened to, and I discovered Irish musicians and the English Premier League. I framed old photographs of John's boyhood — with his father, whom everyone called 'Dennis the Menace', fixing up one of his motorbikes at the rear of his mechanic's workshop; with his pet, Fluffy, the giant white poodle, at the council flat he grew up in; grinning with his brother and sister, clasping a soccer ball tightly to his chest — and displayed them with favourites of my own, such as my father as an eleven-year-old country boy clutching his cricket bat, or my mother's 1940s-era portrait with her two sisters, her short dark-brown hair having been curled in rags for the purpose. Even with contrasting decorative choices our furniture worked when placed together. My square white coffee table, so low to the ground, was a contemporary feat of simple lines that replaced a tired ottoman in the living room and livened up the formerly staid space. John's preference for antiques was reflected in the large items dotted around the house that he had lovingly shipped from London years ago: a cedar sideboard, the glass-fronted bookcase, the chaise longue upholstered in olive-green velvet.

When my upright piano, in hibernation in my parents' garage for too many years, finally took up residence in the broad hallway at the back of the house, I knew my life had changed forever.

As normal as possible, for as long as possible.

As much as I tried to pretend that the details of John's disease were not relevant, the truth of his condition was much less accommodating to our new life than I needed it to be: John was terminally ill. The original diagnosis — after more than a year of increasingly severe lower back pain, one scan was all it took — was an extremely rare tumour of the coccyx, the small triangular bone at the base of the spinal column. To be Latin about it, John had a *coccygeal chordoma*. Despite two major surgeries to excise the primary tumour and its subsequent recurrence, slightly higher this time in the sacrum, the cancer had defiantly returned once more. By the time John and I met, more than three years after he was first diagnosed, the primary tumour had metastasised into secondary bone cancer, taking up residence in the bones of his sacrum, pelvic region and thighs. Having run the medical gamut from two neurosurgeries to bouts of radiotherapy and now chemotherapy, John's treatment options were dwindling rapidly. He had entered the cul-de-sac of palliative care.

John found it difficult at first to accept how much I loved him, and how much I loved his body, twisted and misshapen as it was becoming as a result of the tumours' progress. John's primary tumour protruded about an inch from his sacrum in the shape of a slender baguette about the length of my clenched fist — widest in the middle, tapering off to each side — that sat horizontally across the base of his spine. We are so bombarded with images of strictly defined physical attractiveness that he had long ago disregarded the possibility that anyone would love him again.

'I'm so lucky,' he would say to me.

'*I'm* the lucky one,' I always replied.

It was an odd sensation for me to touch John's tumour at first. It was a body part that I had never imagined existed. It felt the same as touching his nose or his elbow; I was neither turned on or off by it. John's sensation was diminished in his lower back due to his surgeries, so it was far from an erogenous zone for him. There were enough erogenous zones for us to explore. In our first year together we kept ourselves very busy exploring them — in the morning, in the afternoon, before dinner, after dinner — and occasionally surfaced to talk, cook, go to the theatre or the cinema, and attend wine-tasting classes.

One day we lay together as the sun tried its best to sneak through the vines outside into our bedroom. These 'afternoon sessions' were among our favourite pastimes. I looked into John's cornflower-blue eyes and suddenly tears welled in mine.

'Why are you crying?' he said.

'Because I'm so happy,' I said.

We agreed on a guiding principle for the voyage we were embarking on together: that we should try as best we could to live as normal a life as possible, for as long as we possibly could. These words became our mantra, a familiar pattern we repeated to each other when we needed reminding of what was most important. When we began our journey, the horizon seemed years away. As to how many years, neither of us would hazard a guess. Five, perhaps? Maybe ten if things went better than expected. But definitely not two.

I did not think about the fact that John's cancer was terminal.

We were just beginning our life together — the notion of an ending simply did not compute. I could not have been happier unless John had been free of cancer. But we knew that if he had not been sick, he and I might never have met. Our mutual friends had brought us together like two strays who needed a home. And now we were making a new home together. My world grew bigger because John was in it, just as his world changed because I had entered his orbit. Somehow our life became more than the sum of its individual parts. It was such a thrill when friends commented on the energy in the place, on how much they felt at home in our home. I had never felt so at home in my life.

~ဢ

This much was clear from the size of Jim's estimate for the work of drying out my home: the house was facing a fundamental structural problem requiring careful thought, preparation, and detailed attention to correct it.

'Fixing the problem's easy,' Jim told me. 'Preventing the damp from returning is your bigger challenge.'

It turned out that most of the walls of the house would need to be treated. Jim proposed that outside, along the side exposed to the elements, a series of eight metal mesh grilles would be created to allow fresh air to circulate permanently underneath the house. Indoors, the team would begin by drilling two holes into each affected brick in the house. That meant a lot of bricks. Jim hadn't actually mentioned a team. He had said nothing about the number of labourers required for a job of this size. Yet as he described the work involved, I pictured a lithe young gang with blond slacker-style fringes, their taut shoulder blades on display in torn white singlets. After drilling the bricks, the diligent hunks would inject silicone into the holes, then wait for the silicone to dry out the affected bricks. Attention would be paid to these bricks!

That this was the worst case Jim had seen in years made me strangely proud. It felt good to know my rising damp problem was extreme. A relief to have an expert assess the damage and conclude that it was most serious. My home was no run-of-the-mill, simple job that could be sorted out in a fortnight. The process of drying out the house completely — *so you keep the damp from returning, that's what you want*, he said — would take months.

Time. It was going to take time, and fresh air, to help nature provide its own cure. Old-fashioned patience was the thoroughly modern method of treating rising damp. Drying out was beyond the realm of instant gratification. I would simply have to wait.

Although excited by the prospect of how comprehensive this job would be, I remained doubtful. I wasn't sure that it was possible to fix such chronic damp. My fear was not that the rising damp would return, but that it would never go away. These damp walls, this wet-soaked house, were such symbols as my grief was made on. I was living inside a metaphor.

But the thought of all that trapped air being freed was marvellously appealing. I couldn't wait for Jim's team to start work. I wanted those holes drilled into the brickwork immediately. I could picture the damp air, captive for so long, escaping gratefully into the light. Drying from the inside out was exactly what was needed. For my house, and for me.

Part Two

Buried in Work

6

Approaching my front door at the sound of the buzzer, I could see the outline of a tall man through the stained-glass windows. I breathed a sigh of relief. Finally, Jim's team had arrived to begin work on drilling holes into my damp bricks. Waiting for them to start had proven difficult. In the weeks since I had accepted Jim's quote for the work and scheduled the job, the plasterwork seemed to have accelerated its rotting, and the daily evidence of my home's decay — now visible in the walls of the entrance to the house; in the bedroom, where Jim's survey had uncovered yet more damp-ravaged wall space behind the wardrobe and the chest of drawers; and even in the kitchen, where the paint had started peeling away from one wall — was too distressing for someone who was herself imploding. Whoever this man was, he must be the leader of Jim's damp pack.

Opening the door, it seemed as if Gulliver himself was on my doorstep. He was the largest man I had ever seen in close-up, almost six foot six high and at least three feet across the middle. Momentarily I pictured him with branches and a few leaves sprouting from his fingertips. His proportions were such that I literally wouldn't have been able to reach my arms around his trunk. Even if that had been remotely appropriate.

'Hi, I'm Steven,' said the man-mountain. 'Jim sent me.'

He filled my doorframe almost completely and blocked the daylight behind him, so that all this Lilliputian saw was his enormous shadow.

'Oh, yes. Hello. Thanks for coming,' I said, as I opened the security grille and invited him in. 'It's just . . . you?'

I shook the enormous hand Steven had extended in greeting and watched mine disappear.

'Yes, just me I'm afraid,' he smiled, as he slowly crossed my threshold. My melodramatic fantasies of a posse of muscled labourers were at an end. Jim's rising damp 'team' would be just one person, even if he were the size of two regular men. I had to stop myself from laughing out loud: Steven's footsteps might have been heavy, but he had one of the softest male voices I'd ever heard. This was a gentle giant.

After I showed him around the house, Steven wasted no time in getting to work. He crawled his way around my house, inside and out, for more than a week. Steven's voice was but one of several physical paradoxes he displayed while working in my home: he had impressive manoeuvrability for a man with such a huge physical frame. Transfixed, I watched him crouch, bend, kneel, and twist himself around so that one leg was stretched out over the ankle of his other leg, which was bent at the knee. I saw him stand up and sit down quickly, reach high and low. Steven was somehow able to shift his enormous bulk such that he could drill holes in bricks low to the ground, or inside the built-in wardrobe that backed on to an internal wall affected by the rising damp, and move heavy furniture seemingly at the flick of his solid wrist.

Fortunately Steven was oblivious to my voyeurism. He was too busy at ground level to notice anything going on above it. His first task was to dismantle the skirting boards that covered the lowest layers of brick on each internal wall affected by the rising damp. Some of the boards cracked and splintered as he removed them, the timber had rotted so badly; others came away from the wall without a fight. Far from the neatly arranged domestic interior that had greeted him a few days earlier, the inside of my house now resembled a staged demolition site. The skirting boards lay in pieces where he had removed them. Large chunks of plaster fell to the floor in the artful disarray of a still-life painting.

All of Steven's movements seemed unconscious and free from pain. He was blithely ignorant of his physical health. His body revelled in its ability to manipulate itself. I couldn't help but watch him; I was transfixed by his freedom of movement. I cringed to remember how excruciating the least of those movements had become for John in his final months. How standing up, lying down, carrying, hugging, and walking had gradually become impossible due to his spreading tumours and increasing pain. How John's frame, already tiny by comparison to this gentle giant's, was reduced to a skeletal shadow of the body that had once loved running and playing football, riding motorbikes and driving cars, ballroom dancing and making love. In those last months, there was barely anything left of him. John's body deteriorated around him as rapidly as the damp had risen. *Health is a matter of chance*, I thought as I looked at this young labourer drilling away. Dr Atkins himself couldn't prevent his heart attack, despite his vigilant attitude to nutrition and exercise; John's physically active lifestyle provided no credit to set against the mass of cancerous tissue that grew slowly in his coccyx over eighteen months until his diagnosis and surgery to remove it.

Once Steven had detached the skirting boards from the walls, his next task was to drill two equidistant holes into hundreds of individual bricks. His job was twice as big as it first appeared, due to the fact that the walls of my home are double-brick. For each brick the naked eye could see, he had to drill through two bricks to completely penetrate the wall and allow in the fresh air that would start to dry it out. He had to drill in this fashion in most of the rooms of my house, and in most of the walls of each of those rooms. A cloud of fine dust rose in his wake as he lumbered, drill in hand, through the house.

The third step in the process of addressing the rising damp was technically the easiest. Steven injected each of the affected bricks with a silicone-based damp-proofing fluid, shot straight out of a tube that was slotted into a battered mechanism and activated with a trigger. Over time, so the theory goes, the fluid forms a chemical damp-proof course, which prevents the moisture from returning. Watching this man-mountain wander through the hallway with his silicone gun reminded me of Arnold Schwarzenegger in *Terminator*. This rising damp was a more serious enemy combatant than I had ever imagined.

Drilling, penetrating, injecting, fluid: reflecting on the work Steven conducted in my home, it all reads like some B-grade erotic adventure. At the time, however, there was nothing remotely sensuous about the experience. The house was undergoing major work to save it from itself, from the external circumstances that were causing it to rot and decay from the inside out. With its very foundations drilled and its skirting boards hanging off, my house could not have looked more vulnerable. I gazed upon the bare walls, the skirting boards ripped from their former resting places, the ruins of decorative masonry. It was as if my own guts had been ripped out and exposed for all the world to see. The drama of my grief was being played out before my eyes, in my own home.

7

When John first asked me to marry him, he was completely drunk. We had been together for about a month. He had stumbled home late after Friday-night drinks with colleagues, collapsed on the bed and begun telling me how much he loved me.

'Will you marry me, Virginia?' he pleaded. 'Please,' he added after a second, as if politeness itself would cajole me. 'I love you, I want you to marry me. I won't go to sleep until you say you'll marry me,' he declared.

Despite his sloppy delivery, John was insistent. He would not stop badgering me, even as I tried to head back under the covers. 'Of course I'll marry you,' I said eventually, partly to quiet him but charmed in spite of myself.

That was all he needed to hear: he was out like a light.

'Do you remember what you asked me last night?' I said, a little coyly, over breakfast the next morning.

'Asked you? No, I don't remember anything past getting in the front door,' John said.

'You don't remember anything?' I said, disappointed. I wondered whether or not to tell him. After all, I had accepted a marriage proposal uttered by a drunken Irishman just three weeks after said Irishman and I had moved in together.

He shook his head, clearly at a loss. 'What did I say?'

'You asked me to marry you,' I said, very softly.

'I did?' John laughed his gentle chuckle, tilting his chin up slightly. When he laughed his whole face lit up. 'And what did you say?'

I paused. 'I said yes,' I replied, as John's eyes flashed wide in surprise. This was the woman who had recently told him she didn't feel the need to get married. 'But you wouldn't go to sleep unless I answered you, and you were so insistent —'

'I don't believe you! I don't believe you said yes to my drunken proposal. Virginia, what have I done to you?' he said, laughing and shaking his head.

Now I was embarrassed; I had revealed my conscious response to the question his unconscious mind had posed. Later that day I received an email at work with the subject line: *Don't say yes to drunken Irishmen*.

A few months later we started discussing the subject again. This time John was serious. Even better, he was sober. This time he got down on bended knee during one of our barbecues for two on the back deck. This time — for the second time — I accepted.

I had always believed I was the type of woman who would probably never marry. Most men, when it comes to the crunch, don't hurry down the aisle with the intellectual types. Besides, there were very few men I'd met whose merits as a potential husband were clearly evident. The ones whose merits were less than cloudy were inevitably unavailable in one way or another.

The question of whom to marry, and of why two people would marry at all, had always taken precedence over any consideration of the ceremony itself. I was not one of those women who had dreamed of her wedding day since childhood. Hearing about friends' or colleagues' wedding plans was inevitably tedious, even when I strongly believed in the likelihood of a given couple's marriage being a success. What always astounded me was to hear details of the dress or the reception and learn that they had been dreamed of for years, prior to the faintest hope of a husband appearing. Sometimes I wondered if I had missed something because I never played with dolls as a child.

So the prospect of planning our wedding was the equivalent of death by detail. We knew where we wanted to marry — in the garden of our home, surrounded by our loved ones. John wanted a new suit, and control over the selection and purchase of wine for our guests. All I knew was that I didn't want lace, I didn't want to wear an ivory-coloured meringue, and I didn't want a formal reception. I wanted a simple ceremony, a jazz quartet, a lot of fun and very little fuss.

But before we married, we had something else to do first. We had to go on our honeymoon.

As normal as possible, for as long as possible.

There were two reasons for taking a holiday together prior to our November wedding. One was an invitation from one of John's friends to her wedding in the English Cotswolds in September. The other was the advice of John's oncologist, delivered during a July appointment I could not attend to discuss the results of his latest MRI scan.

Interstate for work, I called John to find out what the scans revealed. From his cheerful but guarded response I knew he was holding something back. When I got home that evening, we sat down together on our sofa and held hands as he told me that the cancer had returned. Then he told me he had asked the oncologist how long he had to live.

'He said we should travel as soon as possible.' John paused. 'He thinks I might have less than twelve months.'

The next thing I heard was the sound of someone screaming uncontrollably. It took a second to realise it was me. Although I sat firmly on the couch, an abyss had nevertheless opened up in front of my eyes and I was falling. John, still and calm beside me, tried to comfort me as I howled like a banshee. No matter what I did for John, or how much we loved each other, I realised, he was going to die. But it definitely would not be within twelve months. The oncologist didn't know John as well as I did. How much he wanted to live. We would have a few years together, at least.

~

John wrote to his friends in the UK and Ireland announcing our wedding and pre-emptive European tour. The sprightly tone of his email couldn't disguise the real news of his message.

Well, the words that all cancer patients know are coming at some stage arrived for me last week. The cancer is growing where it had been reduced through radiation or dormant through chemo. The prognosis is poor!

Basically chemo is only likely to have a 20 per cent chance of stalling or shrinking the tumours.

The alternative is radiation — that is problematic as they are unlikely to radiate areas which have already been radiated as the radiation can break down the bones that it comes into contact with. Buggered if they do and buggered if they don't!

I can opt to stop all treatments which would result in a slightly speeded up version of what might happen otherwise. That is, tumours would grow, pain will increase, mobility will diminish, weight will be lost, organs will be affected, and death will follow. How long, is the 64 million dollar question. The Professor indicated that this was very difficult to quantify as the tumours grow differently but slowly and affect different organs singularly and collectively. If pressed he suggested twelve months at a guess.

Virginia and I have two plans — go on the biggest holiday we can, which means the trip is on! The second is to get married on November 29th.

It's been a five-year battle which I have not lost yet but it looks like the enemy is at the gates. I still have plenty of time to do loads of things that I want to and to put as much of the red wine from the cellar into glasses.

I am hoping that the holiday will be fun with as little morbidity as possible.

The oncologist told John that we could expect the disease to progress in the following way: it would decrease John's ability to walk by attacking the thigh bones and pelvic region; then it would affect John's systemic health — his ability to fight infection, his appetite — and finally the tumours would invade his lungs. He explained matter-of-factly that this was a well-established pattern with the type of secondary bone cancer that John had. When the tumours took up residency in his lungs — not if, but when — he would have at best six months to live.

This blunt assessment was accompanied by a farewell handshake and a referral to a specialist at the pain management clinic in the neighbouring building. There would be no more appointments with this doctor, whom John had been visiting for several years. His job was to determine and monitor cancer treatment options. As he made clear, the course of chemotherapy had done little to prevent the spread of John's disease; further radiation of his thigh bones would be counterproductive, causing more damage to the already brittle femurs. Only new sites of tumour could be radiated. There was nothing left in his particular bag of tricks he could use to help John.

~

Shortly before we left for our five-week vacation, John was inducted into the super-strength medications and language of pain management. The oncologist's predictions about John's mobility had been sadly accurate. As we approached the departure date for our honeymoon, John's pain steadily increased. Walking was becoming difficult for any longer than a few minutes, and the pain in his legs worsened considerably at night. Suddenly he needed twenty minutes each morning to move from lying down to sitting up and getting out of bed due to the pain, which shot up and down his legs like arrows.

On our first visit to the pain management clinic, clutching John's referral and what felt like our last straw, a nurse handed him a clipboard with some papers attached and asked him to fill out their patient questionnaire.

Describe your pain. Where is it? Is it always there? Does it spread and, if so, where? When did it start? Is it chronic (ongoing, present for weeks/months/years), constant or intermittent? Are there episodes of more severity? What makes it worse/better? Does it wake you up? Does it interfere with work/activities/relationships? How would you describe its severity on a scale of 0 (no pain) to 10 (worst pain you've ever experienced)? What sort of pain is it? Choose from words like aching, nagging, gnawing, sharp/knife, burning, tingling, uncomfortable, steady, stabbing, shooting, toothache, headache, excruciating.

John dutifully filled out a response to each question in his neat handwriting. I wondered if being a native English speaker put him at a disadvantage. He was too articulate — and too modest — to exaggerate the pain he was in.

It was mid-August, two weeks before we were leaving on our honeymoon. The pain specialist assessed John's medication needs as best he could. But, having just met John and faced with a long and complex medical history to digest, he was reluctant to prescribe anything too powerful. Scribbling incomprehensibly on his prescription pad, the specialist explained that the new medication regime he was prescribing for John was designed to address the two separate types of pain he was experiencing — pain caused directly by the cancer itself; and neuropathic (nerve) pain caused by the primary tumour pressing on John's spine and sending his nervous system haywire. Within a couple of weeks of trial and trauma, however, it was clear to both of us that the medication was inadequate to the task and we returned to the specialist desperate for more help before we flew out of the country. We were beginning to discover that the process of titrating new medicines to the correct dose and frequency, experimenting with each drug and trying to determine its efficacy as well as its side-effects, and identifying the benefits and disadvantages of any one medication in isolation, involved as much art as it did science. Sometimes it took weeks or months to get right. For those, like John, who are in extreme pain, the pain doesn't ever really go away. It is just *managed*.

———⌒౨

At Los Angeles International Airport, that corral of tired long-haul travellers manhandled by an overzealous army of underpaid immigration officials, I stood in the queue labelled Citizens and Permanent Residents and waited to hand in the final documentation that triggered the issuing of my green card. John joined the long queue for temporary visitors. A stern airport immigration officer took my Consulate-endorsed papers and then my photograph. He held my right hand and pressed my index finger and thumb into an ink pad. Again. I had lost count of the number of times the US Government had documented my fingerprints. After ten minutes I was, technically speaking, a permanent resident of the United States.

I waited for John at the baggage carousel and wondered what on earth I was doing. I was on my honeymoon. I wasn't even married yet and here I was, completing the paperwork for the option of a future life that would not include John, my husband-to-be.

I was on my honeymoon months before my wedding, because my fiancé might not be able to walk by the time we married.

New York was no longer somewhere I wanted to live, but after a six-year absence Manhattan was like a wonderful old friend I couldn't wait to introduce to John. At a friend's suggestion we had booked into the SoHo Grand Hotel for their 'Sex in the City' package, which offered a discount for four nights' stay and included breakfast. Unfortunately John was in so much pain as a result of our long-haul flight there was next to no sex at all. We took each day slowly because we had to, and at night ate in cafes close to the hotel. Yet we managed to see a lot. In five days we packed in a trip on the Staten Island Ferry, a visit to the Empire State Building, a Guggenheim Museum exhibition, a jazz club, a night out at the theatre, and a few old favourite haunts like the Empire Diner and Raoul's. We hailed taxis to minimise the amount of walking John had to do. He took dozens of photographs with the semi-professional quality digital camera he had bought months earlier. 'You're so at home here,' he told me.

Our second stop was Ireland, where a well-meaning friend of John's took us out on Dublin Harbour in his small speedboat for a dramatic change of pace and scene from New York's urban jungle. It certainly was dramatic. After we had been on the water for about twenty minutes I became aware of the sudden onset of a strong wind, which had whipped the water into stiff peaks. The boat literally collided into each wave in order to progress through the water. We were jolted forward and back in our seats every time the little boat slammed up and into a new wave and then landed heavily on the other side of it. I looked across at John, feeling sick with the knowledge of what this relentless pattern was doing to his lower back. He looked at me and shook his head, imploring me to say nothing, to do nothing. He winced. It was all he could do not to cry out in agony. We were far from shore and had no choice but to endure the trip back to the marina in pain and silence. But by the time we were on dry land again it was too late. The damage was done.

John never really recovered from that boat trip, and pain remained our third wheel for the duration of our honeymoon. For the next three weeks, which we spent in northern Italy and the UK, John downed eight Panadols a day to complement his morphine tablets, which were insufficient to combat his physical distress. (On our first visit to the pain specialist after we returned, the doctor tripled the dose.) John was shocked at the sudden intensification of pain, and at its practical consequences. I was also shocked at how quickly our holiday had become compromised by John's pain, but focused on practical ways in which I could help ameliorate his daily agony. Each morning I gave him a couple of Panadols when he woke up, giving him time to adjust to conscious pain and to help his body relax enough so that he could get out of bed. Because it was too painful now for him to bend, I had to help him into and out of the shower, and to put his socks and shoes on for him and tie his shoelaces. Soon it was taking as long as one and a half hours from the time John woke up to being showered and dressed. It was clear that he desperately required much stronger pain-relieving medication, but on our vacation we had no means of acquiring it.

In those stretches of time when John felt better — hours, sometimes a whole afternoon — we enjoyed ourselves like any other couple who were madly in love. In Dublin we explored Trinity College and I tried my first Guinness. We wandered around Parma, a postcard-perfect town in northern Italy, taking photographs and people-watching from cafes. We visited hill-top towns whose fortifications dated back centuries, and ate our way through the provincial specialities of Emilia-Romagna. In London we held hands and walked through Kenwood House in Hampstead, and even went on a tour of Windsor Castle.

Towards the end of our holiday, we celebrated the second wedding of John's friend Elizabeth in the picturesque Cotswolds. Elizabeth's first husband, who had died in his early forties from cancer, had been a close friend of John's. John had already been through his first operation to excise the original tumour before Peter had started experiencing his first symptoms. Between Peter's diagnosis and death were just eight short months. In addition to losing her husband, Elizabeth had also lost the father of their two young children. Now, two years after she had been widowed, she was marrying Robert, someone Elizabeth and her late husband had known as a friend for a long time. The first part of the ceremony was very moving. Robert formally asked Elizabeth's children, in front of all of us — including the dead man's parents — if they would like him to be their daddy from now on. Fortunately the children smiled and nodded their assent. I squeezed John's hand and tried to remember whether my mascara was waterproof. I looked from them to John and down to our clasped hands, feeling as if I were about to jump off a cliff. The man beside me would soon be my husband, and I knew already that at some future moment I would be his widow. And that he and I would have no children together.

~ᘓ

On our return to Sydney, John began using a walking stick to take the pressure off his right leg. The stick had been lying around the house since he had used it as part of his recovery from the second major surgery a few years earlier. The wooden stick was plain and elegant. I thought John looked very dignified using it.

One week later, he called me at work, uncharacteristically agitated, and asked me to come home. He had been talking with a former colleague who was visiting, and had leaned forward as he sat on the sofa to reach for a biscuit on the coffee table. As he bent over his hips, he felt something give way and jolted forward, suddenly off-balance, and fell to the floor in acute pain.

Although diagnosis took a few weeks, that accident caused a hairline fracture to John's pelvic bone, a region of his body into which the original tumour in his sacrum had metastasised during the year. The fracture showed that he could no longer bear any weight on his right leg due to the extent of disease in that thigh bone.

'Doc says I'm going to have to use crutches now,' he said when he called me at work after the doctor's home visit that confirmed the diagnosis.

'What do you mean?' I said. 'You're already using the walking stick.'

'No, darling,' he said. 'I have to use two crutches. My left leg can't bear all the weight of the right leg anymore, it's not strong enough.'

John delivered this news in the tone of someone reporting a trip to the grocery store that had failed to procure an important item.

I'll have to use rocket instead of continental parsley for the garnish. It's all right.

'But this is a temporary thing, isn't it?' I said, not comprehending.

He paused. 'No, it's permanent.' He must have wondered how he could make the news any clearer to his dim fiancée.

I'll have to use crutches instead of my legs to walk. It's all right.

'Oh, John, really?' I said, slightly irritated, as if he'd told me he had forgotten to take out the garbage.

It was three days before the wedding. My first thought was how ungainly the crutches would look in our photographs. Everything was organised. Our vows, which we had written ourselves, were neatly typed. The menu of finger food had been decided after discussions with the caterers about vegetarians and an assessment of the likelihood of implosion in the guests' hands of certain menu items. The jazz quartet that would provide the soundtrack to our celebration had been sent the music and a recording of the song we wanted them to play as I walked through the house to the garden. Despite my will to power, the music chosen was not Handel's 'Arrival of the Queen of Sheba', but a simple and affecting composition by South African pianist Abdullah Ibrahim, called 'The Wedding'. I was cranky. Crutches were not part of the plan. John used an unobtrusive and dignified walking stick. Crutches were ugly and obvious. Crutches would ruin everything.

8

While I had attended a Christmas and Easter mass with John, I had grown up in the Protestant tradition and knew nothing of the rituals or vocabulary of the Catholic church. Neither had I any understanding of how the wheels of death turned. Nobody close to me had died. All my grandparents were gone by the time I was four years old, so I had no experience of funeral bureaucracy. No understanding of when or how the funeral home knew to take John's body from Canterbury Hospital, or how to book a church for a memorial service. It was a mystery to me who took care of the newspaper notice, or who identified John's pallbearers. Who would speak at the funeral and what they would say. If it was expected of the widow to speak. What she would say.

I called John's church and to my surprise received a recorded message. 'For mass times, press one. To speak to a priest, press two. For all other matters . . .' Finally I spoke to the receptionist and asked her to put me through to John's priest. I had met him once or twice when he came to the house to talk to John, but their conversations, occurring as they did just a couple of weeks before his death, took place in private.

'It's his day off,' she said.

Does God know? I thought. I wondered what a priest would do on his day off. Tear off his collar, pick up women, race around on a motorbike honking his horn and screaming at the top of his lungs? Maybe he just does his laundry like the rest of us.

~

When the priest visited the next day, he seemed very shy. Sheila was able to put him at ease because she could speak Catholic. We were determined that the service be a celebration of John's life, not any more sorrowful than it had to be. I had heard a grown man burst into tears over the phone when I asked him to be a pallbearer: I did not need any further *evidence* of how people who knew John felt about losing him.

With the detached impersonal attention of a bureaucrat, the priest showed us some books and talked us through the Catholic funeral service. The short version. He left the books for Sheila and me to look through — *you might like to ask a few people to say a eulogy or to read a verse you select*, he said, before he left. I wondered on what criteria I might *select* a reading. I felt that I was being asked to conduct a performance comprising diverse elements with a consistent theme, but with no knowledge of the music, the players, or the audience. Sheila seemed to know what was required. After all, she had had to do all of this for her own mother five years earlier, and for her father a few years before that.

~

The funeral home sent a Nice Young Man to guide me through the labyrinth of their arrangements. He was the first of many people to do a brief double-take when he saw me. I suppose one imagines widows to have grey hair and a creased forehead. Even if you meet new ones every week.

I couldn't believe how many concrete decisions were required of the next of kin. The grieving party. The bereaved. The widow. The words I would like included in the newspaper notice. The clothes I wanted John to be buried in. The floral arrangement I wanted on top of the casket. The sort of wood from which the casket should be made. The youthful funeral director helpfully opened his presentation folders to show me the latest looks in caskets.

I didn't *want* any of it, I wanted to tell the nice young man. I didn't *care* what sort of wood the casket was made from. I didn't *mind* what arrangement sat on top of it. John didn't care about flowers that much anyway. He always bought me a bottle of wine instead of a bouquet. If we must have flowers on top, so be it. I didn't have the energy to question it. It just couldn't look *cheap*. I could cope with anything except *tacky*. He showed me photographs of possible floral tributes, each protected by a plastic sleeve. What were they being protected from? Clumps of my wet tissue. Snot. Heartache.

As Sheila and I spoke to the funeral director, I kept confusing my vocabulary. I said 'wedding' when I meant 'funeral'. It didn't happen once or twice. I had already said it to the priest, to a nurse, and to my parents. Only their shocked expressions alerted me to the fact I had misspoken. My verbal confusion happened on a handful of occasions during this first meeting with the funeral director. I even substituted 'honeymoon' for 'burial' at one point. The words bubbled out of me, making the connections by themselves. The two events had occurred within the space of a year, irrationally close to each other. It was too easy for my unconscious to connect the dots.

Of all the decisions I had to make in the first few days, the one I had no trouble with was choosing the clothes that John would be buried in. He would wear the black Hugo Boss suit he looked so handsome in when he married me on our wedding day, eleven months ago. The fact that I knew which clothes John would be buried in did not mean that I *wanted* John to be buried in them. I didn't want John to be buried at all. I wanted him to tell me where he was so I could collect him and bring him back home. I went straight to the cupboard and put the whole outfit into a bag for the nice young funeral director to take with him — the Italian white cotton shirt we bought on our pre-wedding European tour; the burnished gold tie that perfectly matched the colour of my dress; John's favourite dress shoes, polished to a bright shine.

Composing the public funeral notice had proven more difficult than I expected. And despite my attention to editorial detail, its publication was a disaster. Somehow, between my composition of the words and the funeral home's communication with the newspaper, not only syntax but social order had been perverted. The *Sydney Morning Herald* listed Sheila as John's mother, and misspelled his mother's name, Celia, as Cheila, who was listed as his sister. Having spent childhood weekend mornings watching my mother turn first to the column she dubbed 'hatches, matches, catches and dispatches', I knew this was one piece of biographical information about my husband that total strangers would read. I imagined them pausing at the names Sheila and Cheila, thinking, 'A rhyming family. How peculiar.'

9

The garden at the back of our home was the obvious setting for our wedding. We spent many hours there entertaining friends or whiling away afternoons and evenings by ourselves. The space was lush with green leaves and luxuriant shrubs, and a border of tall lilly pilly trees offered privacy and seclusion from the apartment block next door. The covered deck would provide enough shelter for the musicians we had hired, and the large fig tree at the bottom of the garden was the perfect place in front of which John and I would exchange our vows.

We had drawn up a list of people to invite and split them into two camps: domestic and international. Even after seven years away from England, John had maintained close friendships with people living there, and with others who had moved to other countries for work. He was confident that next to none of them would make the long journey to Australia.

'Oh, he won't come,' John said when I asked who a particular guest was. 'He's too busy with work.' Of another couple he said, 'They *definitely* won't come — they've got children.'

They all accepted our invitation. In the end we welcomed twelve international guests, who flew in from London, Dublin, Hong Kong, Seoul, and Auckland. Most of them I had never met. Others I had met for the first time on our honeymoon a few months earlier. It was so wonderful to see John surrounded by his old friends. He had underestimated how happy they were for him.

It had rained all week, but on Saturday, 29 November, the day of our wedding, the sun shone brightly and by the afternoon it was very warm. At my parents' house I put on my bronze silk dress, a simple but flattering v-neck design that cinched at the waist and fell gently to my ankles, and the sandals that by some miracle perfectly matched the colour of my dress.

The only hiccup in preparation was my hair and makeup artist, who was almost one hour late. My brother had already taken my mother to our house to join the other guests by the time she turned up. My father had steam coming out of his ears — patience is not his strong point — but even that didn't faze me.

'You're the calmest bride I have ever seen,' she said as she put the finishing touches on my face.

~

I will never forget the feeling of walking through our house and out into the garden, to be greeted by our friends and family. *This is my tribe*, I remember thinking when I saw their expectant faces light up as I walked towards them. Overwhelmed, my heart leapt into my mouth and I fought back tears. I tried to move slowly and take in every detail, but it was impossible. John was waiting for me at the end of my walk, and I couldn't wait a moment longer to become his wife. He was so peaceful as I walked towards him. His crutches were propped against a nearby chair; he stood unaided and very still. He was exactly where he wanted to be, and so was I. As he smiled and took my hands in his, I knew I was home.

'Will you love and respect him, trust his word, care for him and stand by him, whatever the future may hold?' the celebrant asked me. She had no idea that John and I, as well as most of our guests, knew all too well what the future would hold.

'I will,' I said, my lower lip trembling. I looked at my parents in the front row of white chairs we had hired. They had recently celebrated forty years of marriage. 'That's longer than life in prison!' my father liked to joke. But after sharing so much of their lives together, he and my mother were halves of the same whole. For better and for worse.

Our vows hadn't seemed so difficult to utter when John and I first wrote them. 'I promise that for as long as we shall live, I will cherish the time we have together,' I repeated, shaking my arms in John's to stop me from weeping. 'My love will give you strength to face the future, no matter how hard it might become.' He was the one who three days ago had learned he would need crutches to keep walking, but it was I who needed his support.

No one present that day imagined I would be a widow before our first anniversary.

~

On our wedding day John did remarkably well to disguise the fact he had started using crutches; they appear in only one or two photographs. Around the house, as he learned to use the crutches, he teetered and tottered, walking in an exaggerated stilted fashion like Frankenstein's monster. 'These fucking sticks!' he called them. Sometimes, as we cuddled on the sofa or ate dinner by candlelight in the dining room, where the mood lighting hid the mould spores spreading across the walls, I was often surprised by the sight of our uninvited guests. At night the crutches stood guard like sentinels by John's side of the bed. Too big and unwieldy to be anyone's permanent companions, they usually signify a temporary mobility impairment. But these crutches were John's new legs.

One morning shortly after we were married, John nudged open our bedroom door. He was never the first one out of bed anymore, even though his newest mix of medications seemed to be keeping the pain under control for now. The first cup of tea every morning was one of our rituals, and I was the one who made it. Somehow, using two crutches to remain upright, John had not only prepared me a cup of tea, but transported it from the kitchen at the back of our home to our bedroom at the front. I looked at John, his face full of concentration. Some tea spilled over the sides of the teacup and swilled around in the saucer. But it wasn't tea that I saw. It was love.

10

'Don't wear black, I don't want you to wear black,' John had told me. He could hardly breathe to get the words out, but he insisted. So I wore a dusty pink v-neck dress to my husband's funeral. My concession to the conventional colour of widowhood was in my matching black shoes and hat. I felt I needed a hat. I'm not sure why. Sheila took me into David Jones to look for the items I felt were necessary. Shopping was not a distraction, it was purposeful. I knew what items I needed, and I was determined to find them.

The shoes were easy enough. But downstairs in the hat department, it was a fight to the death. Having lost all sense of time and the national calendar, I was unaware until that moment that it was just a few days before the Melbourne Cup.

In the midst of this sophisticated melee I looked for a small, elegant, black hat of plain design. The task was proving difficult not just because of the crowd but for the style I needed. After what seemed like twenty minutes of futile search, I saw a design I knew would suit me — a small plain hat with a slightly angled top, a short but downwards-tilting brim, and an elegant thin bow at the back. No one else was interested in the hat because it was the antithesis of the kind of flamboyant style required for a day at the races. My hat was perfect but for one important thing: it was chocolate brown.

I approached a sales assistant, one of many deluged by impatient customers waiting to make their purchase for race day.

'Do you have this hat in black?' I asked her, keeping my tone light and evenly modulated. I felt like I was speaking a foreign language.

She looked at the plain hat I was holding and pursed her lips. 'Oh, well, maybe somewhere out the back, but . . .' She shrugged, indicating that now was not the time to be digging around in storage for another version of this poor cousin of a hat.

'Couldn't you take a look? Please?' I said. 'I need it today. I need it. I have to wear it to . . . to my husband's funeral.'

It was the first time I had said those words out loud. Immediately I collapsed in Sheila's arms and began sobbing; I thought I would never stop. *My husband's funeral.* Such an elegant phrase. Brutally concise. I had seen that phrase in print before; I had heard actors on stage and on screen use those words in that order. But to describe my bleak goal so precisely, to a stranger, for the purpose of a transaction, was too much.

The sales assistant knew she could make a difference. While Sheila helped me to regain some composure, the assistant returned a few minutes later with the hat, in black. The Melbourne Cup shoppers, their curiosity piqued, probably felt a little ashamed of the woman who became hysterical over a hat. I wanted to do something extraordinary for the sales assistant. She was only doing her job, but at that moment it was the most important thing anyone could have done for me. Later, when I thought of bringing her some flowers to say thank you, I realised I had no idea what she looked like.

—☙

On the day of the funeral the weather could have only been described as Irish. John would have been delighted at the relentless heavy downpour. He was always worried about Sydney's notorious water shortages. I thought of the windswept Julie Christie in *Far From the Madding Crowd* as an appropriately melodramatic double. A fictionalised version of myself was easier to imagine than the reality of my present.

My parents and brother came over to the house as Sheila and I finished getting ready. The funeral car would arrive shortly to take us the short distance to St Fiacre's, the church at the top of our street. It was a short walk, but the driving rain made walking out of the question. My jersey dress hung about me; I didn't realise I had lost so much weight. Pulling on pantyhose, stepping into my heels, applying lipstick and mascara: it all seemed impudent. But I was representing John and I had a job to do.

We waited for the funeral car, but it failed to arrive. It never occurred to me that a widow and her posse could be stood up on the occasion of her husband's funeral. My brother jumped into action, making two trips around the block in his small car so all of us could make it in time. Being late to my own wedding was one thing. To be late to my husband's funeral was out of the question.

I had no idea who would be there, how many people might attend. I was moving through this day in a cloud of other people's sorrow, trying hard to stay upright. The funeral gave others the opportunity to gather on John's behalf, to celebrate his life. To me it felt like an official event that needed to be performed and completed.

At the church, strangers signed their names in the book of attendance. I looked at faces with a glazed expression, not recognising them. There were people in attendance who had known John for a lot longer than I had. Several people had made the effort to come to the funeral in the teeming rain, when a single phone call or an email while John was alive had somehow proven too difficult.

Sheila, my parents, my brother and I all sat together in the front row, close to the casket with the obligatory flowers displayed across it. I concentrated very hard on the sound of my own breathing. It felt surreal to be inside a church, even if it was the one closest to home. As the priest spoke kindly about John, I paid attention to his every word, yet heard nothing. I wondered if he was disappointed I wasn't Catholic. If he had visions of John in purgatory because he had been divorced. Or of me eventually burning in hell for sins such as getting married in the garden of our home instead of in this ornately decorated hall. I remember clenching my calf muscles and splaying my fingers during the service as John's closest friends and colleagues spoke of his love of work, of wine, of wife. I had composed some words to say, and to my surprise I wasn't daunted by the prospect of reading them out. To speak to this group of friends and strangers was to deliver a message on John's and my behalf. My only doubt was whether my legs would carry me when the time came to stand up. They felt as foreign to me as those of a newborn foal.

~

The memorial service was not without its surprises. About ten minutes into proceedings, a slight commotion from the back of the church unsettled the priest. People began shifting in their seats and craning their necks to see what was happening. I had not turned around, but I recognised the voice immediately.

'Dio! Dio! Johnny, Dio!'

Connie and Frank, our neighbours who lived across the street, were latecomers to the service. Usually they attended the Italian-language masses. Connie wailed loudly as she struggled down the aisle towards the front, hands outstretched towards John's coffin, oblivious to the mourners already gathered. She had managed to bring the priest to a halt, mid-sentence. Frank, bringing up the rear on his walking stick, couldn't catch up with his wife, who had gathered momentum as she neared the front of the church.

'Johnny, Johnny, aaagh! Dio, mio Dio,' she shrieked, laying her hands on the rosewood box.

They were loud and oblivious to the rest of us, and they interrupted the order of service, but their sorrow was undeniable. To our collective relief, another neighbour who knew them got up and ushered them into a nearby pew.

Afterwards, outside in the heavy rain, I received dozens of embraces in the same way the Queen accepts bouquets of flowers from strangers. Nodding and approximating a smile for each person who approached me, their faces twisted in sorrow, I appreciated their hugs and kisses but was removed from the gestures, as if it were someone else the mourners embraced. A friend held a large umbrella over my head as I stood outside the church, but I was somewhere else entirely.

~

At the gravesite we stood on artificial grass under a small marquee. Even now I can't recall whether there were fifteen or forty of us. The rain did not let up, but there were plenty of those enormous black umbrellas to keep us all dry. Those funeral directors think of everything. The bright green plastic grass surrounded the rectangular hole that had been dug. Plot number 943 on the map, just like I'd ordered.

I was neither a Catholic nor did I have experience of burials. But I had read plenty of Thomas Hardy as a melancholic teenager.

I watched as the priest read from his prayer book, and looked around at those who had made the sodden journey from St Fiacre's to the cemetery. I remember wondering if the priest was bothered by the rain, and how often he had to conduct this ceremony in extreme weather. Or even extreme boredom. Certainly his vestments, soaked with rain, clung sadly about him; he seemed sanguine about being so wet. Only his face was dry. I envied him his faith.

I looked at Sheila, sobbing away, and realised I was not. I didn't shed a single tear at the cemetery. I must have been in shock. A ceremony was unfolding in a preordained sequence but I did not notice, so mesmerised was I by the rain and the priestly incantations, until Sheila offered me a wreath of flowers she had picked up the previous afternoon and motioned me to join her. I didn't know what I was supposed to do. Only as I shuffled towards her did I see that the coffin was being lowered into the ground.

The priest opened his book and said a few more words. Sheila nudged me gently to lay the wreath upon the coffin. I moved forward a few steps and was stunned to see men in black suits levering the rosewood box into a deep hole that had been dug in preparation. These men were *working*, manoeuvring the coffin using a series of thick canvas belts and pulleys to gradually lower it into the wet ground. Like the umbrellas, these burly men in matching black suits seemed to have appeared out of nowhere, but later I concluded they must have doubled as the drivers of the funeral cars.

I knelt down and placed the flowers on top of the coffin. It felt as though I were acting in someone else's drama. But at that moment, under the marquee, it struck me that this was no performance. It didn't make sense that the dead body of my husband was lying inside that box, dressed as he had been on the day he married me not quite eleven months ago. It didn't make sense that I was standing beside it, wearing a black hat and a pink dress, holding more useless flowers to throw over him. None of it made sense, yet it was happening. I remember a feeling of slight concussion, that I was not actually there in the moment, but somewhere just behind it or in front of it. Not *in* it. Not actually *present* to fully experience the act of John's burial. But being *forced* to see it nonetheless.

Once the coffin was in the ground I didn't know whether there was more to come from the priest, or whether I was supposed to mingle with people beneath the small tent. After a minute or two, I said suddenly to the group of mourners, 'Come on, let's go — he'd think we were a bunch of eejits for standing around in this weather.' It was entirely true, and people smiled at me. I could see that they agreed with me but also admired the brave young widow for being honest about the hideous conditions. And so people started to move off down the slippery grass verge towards the comforts of bitumen and their friends' cars. I don't remember whether I wanted to stay longer and pretended otherwise for the sake of those present, or whether I wanted to disappear as quickly as possible from the cemetery and if that meant everyone having to leave when I did, then so be it. Sometimes I worry that my domineering common sense curtails moments of great emotion. But at this moment, with my husband newly interred, I had had enough emotion. There was nothing I could express in this particular public that was not already written clearly on my face. I must have thanked the priest and received condolences beneath the artificial canopy, but I have no recollection of it.

At home in our absence, the caterer had been hard at work cutting the crusts off slices of bread and making platters of sandwiches. My mother had hired her for the job because she specialised in 'bereavement catering'. By the lines on her face she'd seen her fair share of wakes. I looked at the elegant trays of sandwiches and wondered whether by removing the crusts she had intended to soften our collective blow. Or if a less muscular action of the mouth, in the act of chewing, was associated somehow with a proper level of respect for the dead.

Mum had trouble convincing her that I was the widow. 'But she only looks twenty-five!' the old woman exclaimed in my earshot, with a rueful shake of her head. Evidently death became me.

The rain dripped on John's bereft work colleagues — the small team had worked together since a few weeks after he had first moved to Australia — as we stood on the back deck under its leaking corrugated roof. *I really have to get that fixed*, I thought. We chatted for a while, listening politely to each other's stories. The last time all these people had been standing around inside and outside the house had been our wedding day. I barely knew these men and women but I loved them for their fierce loyalty to John. I looked around the garden, the leaves and branches heavy and glistening with the weight of water upon them. This had been our sanctuary, our leafy refuge from the world. We had talked for hours out here, solving the world's problems over coffee and glasses of wine. There was only ever one problem for which we had no solution. Suddenly the garden felt overgrown. *I must prune the vines and unnecessary branches.* The old wooden palings of the fence were caving in, leaning into each other like an old couple sitting on a bench. *Time for a new fence, too.*

When everyone had left, I was astonished to discover that not a single sandwich remained. Do we eat to forget, I wondered, or to remind ourselves we are still alive?

Part Three

Domesticus Interruptus

11

Patience had paid off: the house had completely dried out. The salty mineral deposits had worked their way out of the brickwork as it dried, just as Jim told me they would. There were no more small mounds of dust gathering each week on my living room floor as the excess moisture's effects on the rotting plasterwork had been arrested. The rising damp had been unequivocally defeated.

Over the months that the damp took to dry out, I passed a lot of time at home in frenzied bouts of domestic activity. The drilled walls exhibited a quiet patience I could not always match. The sense of security I found within the familiar contours of my home was tempered by my compulsion to empty out its every drawer, identify every item that had lain undisturbed for years, and shed the things that no longer belonged. Room by room, I stripped the surfaces of my home of their contents. Framed photographs, books, and the occasional vase were all that was left on display. I had upturned every item that had sat undisturbed on shelves, or rested inside cupboards, and ruthlessly determined its fate. Whatever wasn't bolted to the floor was at risk of being jettisoned. Out went the CDs I would never listen to and the Atari arcade game John had faithfully kept for years behind the door to his study, where it was only used as a surface for dust and unfiled documents. Contrary to my expectations I could not muster sentimental feelings over John's old address books or photographs of people I did not recognise — they also went the way of all trash. I curated a small selection of photographs of John's parents and sent the rest to Sheila in Dublin. Although still unwilling to say goodbye to many of John's clothes, I left bags full of his business socks, rolled neatly into pairs, and boxer shorts on my doorstep for St Vincent de Paul to collect.

I created this domestic routine because the vacuum of the empty home was too large for me to fill by sitting still. Late at night I sometimes wandered into each room, looking around at the architectural details — the roses in the high ceilings, the picture rails, the rust-stained floorboards — yearning for the house to speak to me like a lover. I talked to a gust of wind, which blew through the security door and sent the silk wall-hanging in the living room fluttering, as if it were my husband. I reminded myself that John wanted me to remember all our happy times. I did: that was the problem.

The last Sunday of every month was marked in red felt pen on my calendar. On this day the local council encouraged us to dispense with unnecessary household items and leave them on the pavement for them to collect and dump on our behalf. But I needed no encouragement. Over time I placed so many items I no longer wanted on the footpath outside my house — broken saucepans, crockery, tins of old paint, dog-eared paperbacks, even the shelves on which some of the books had sat — that my address became a reliable destination for that happy band of gleaners who trawl the streets prior to council clean-up day. As the months passed, I became convinced that my street had been listed on a 'best-of' website for people whose treasure was my trash.

After six months of forensic exhumation of my home's every dusty corner, there was nothing left to give away, and I had nothing more to give. I had emptied the house of all but the essentials, until all that remained was a skeleton, devoid of flesh and feeling. My domestic archeology was complete.

~

During the initial work to attack the damp, I had lined up another Irishman, Jack — a mate of Jim's — to render the internal and external walls when the house was ready. Dried out, with its internal surfaces cleared of all items and its foundations breathing fresh air, it was time to cover up the drilled bricks with a coat of plaster. To create a smooth finish, ready for painting. A surface so immaculate that the innocent eye would find it impossible to believe that these walls had ever been anything other than smooth, unmediated, intact.

I learned that applying the render was only the first step. Like any skin treatment, in order to achieve a smooth outer layer, the initial application of render would have to be polished to a smooth finish. Jack would not only apply the walls' new surface: he would exfoliate it too. He warned me there would be a fine layer of dust on every surface. The fresh air that had carried away the dampness of my double-bricks would this time deposit fine particles of plaster everywhere from my lingerie drawer to the keys of my piano. It would inveigle its way into the stereo, the television and the computer, into my books and the buttons on my remote control. It would be so comprehensive in its coverage, Jack said, that he recommended I leave the house for the week it would take him to complete his work.

The prospect of being away from the house during this time didn't bother me. I knew it would be in safe hands and receiving the professional help it needed. With all the intimate knowledge of my home, and the effort I had invested in its contents over the months to this point, I knew the house could take any challenge. It had withstood so much already. It had nothing to fear from Jack the Renderer.

My parents helped me remove all the remaining items displayed on open surfaces — mantelpiece, kitchen bench, chest of drawers, desk — and cover up the furniture and bookcases and electrical equipment with old sheets and towels. With the addition of Jack's own drop sheets to cover the wooden floorboards and the carpet in the bedrooms, the interior of my home was completely transformed. It was as if a dramatic snowfall inside the house had made the once familiar contours of my home unrecognisable. Now it was a huge, empty cavern defined only by the walls and decorative fixtures not hidden by drop sheets. A photographer might have called it *negative space*.

12

A few weeks after John died I decided to return to work. Just two weeks after I had buried him, and eleven months after our wedding. A newlywed newly widowed.

Deciding to go back to the office was the result of a process of elimination. I simply didn't know what else to do with myself. At the time, my options seemed to be either to sit around and look at the damp-damaged walls; to hide beneath the bedcovers; to sprawl on the sofa and try to read; or somehow to do nothing at all. There were problems with each of these options: sitting around and looking at the walls reminded me of how bad I had let the damp get; bed was the last place I could find sleep, and made me hyper-conscious of being alone in it; reading was impossible — I couldn't concentrate to flip through a magazine, let alone to read a book — and the wretched offerings of daytime television held no appeal. Roaming around the house, crying, drinking tea, staring into space, and opening sympathy cards made me feel more aimless than I already was. I didn't want to go anywhere further than my local shops, but neither did I want to stay at home for long days just waiting for them to stretch into even longer nights. To remain at home was not going to help me. Privacy wasn't the issue: I could cry anywhere. The supermarket aisle, the local park, the roundabout at the top of my street that served to remind me I was driving back to an empty house. By the time two weeks had nudged towards three, I knew for certain that no matter how many tears I shed in these early days of widowhood, the hardest challenges for me lay in the foggy realm of the months to come.

Thanks to the overriding Protestant work ethic of my parents, I am genetically incapable of doing nothing. While it's always easy to blame one's parents for one's own faults, it was less shocking to do that than to admit the sorts of unreasonable expectations I made of myself during these first weeks. My husband was dead, and I was worrying about what to *do*. My chest burned from the hole in my heart, but I wondered how to keep myself *busy*. I hoped desperately that returning to work would provide me with a sense of routine, and that routine would, in and of itself, help. Surely adopting the shared public timetable of nine-to-five, Monday-to-Friday working hours would provide me with some relief. I had performed to that timetable before. Surely I could do it now.

So one Tuesday morning I got up, brushed my teeth, showered, dressed and headed out. Given my general sleeplessness and my distorted sense of time, I immediately realised there was no hope of my adhering *strictly* to the nine-to-five schedule. Often it was five o'clock in the morning before I drifted off to sleep, making an early morning start impossible. On this morning it was closer to ten o'clock that I walked along the short path to the front gate, paused, and took a deep breath. I was afraid to open the gate. It felt like embarking on a story that might never end. Stepping out into the street, I closed the gate behind me and walked slowly down the road and around the corner to the bus stop on Parramatta Road.

As I approached the bus stop, my senses seemed to be working overtime. The planes descending towards the airport had never seemed quite so loud, or the hum of traffic so noisy; the screech of trucks changing gear roared between my ears. Moving sluggishly along the footpath I began to notice the other commuters, who were standing quietly waiting for their bus. They were sipping coffee, reading the newspaper, playing with their mobile phones. They seemed completely unaware that anything had changed.

The bus arrived. My heart was pounding as I got on board, although it felt lodged in my throat. I was relieved to find a seat. Without one I was afraid I might faint. During the commute I kept myself busy by concentrating hard on breathing, rummaging for non-existent items inside my handbag, and trying not to make any eye contact with another passenger.

I almost burst with relief as I exited the bus at my usual stop. I had just successfully accomplished my first bus ride in this brave new world without John in it. But no sooner had I allowed myself to feel this small achievement, I was pummelled on all sides by people: rushing in every direction, shouting into their phones, buying this, selling that. One man had the temerity to be collecting funds for cancer research. Alone in this sea of strangers, my eyes welled with disappointment and rage. I felt violated by the sensory overload. The city looked to be open for business. *As usual*.

Making it as far as the lobby of my office tower was the next stage in this pilgrim's progress. In the elevator to my floor I jiggled my arms and legs and tilted my neck from side to side, as if I were loosening up for a title fight. Despite my attempts at invisibility, my small team, who were expecting me, smiled warmly with sad eyes. They were waiting for a sign. I smiled back. *It's all right*, my smile told them, *my edifice will not collapse in front of you*. After a minute I retreated to my own workspace, shut the door and let out a monumental sigh. I had made it into work. Today I had accomplished something.

It hadn't yet occurred to me that at some point I would have to do more than just turn up. And that I would have to do this again tomorrow. Get up, brush my teeth, get on the bus, go to work. And then the day after that. Get on the bus, go to work, *do* some work. To keep producing work, to keep *performing*, as part of my employment contract. As part of the broader social contract, whose terms none of us signed but all understand. In times of crisis I often heard Macbeth's words tolling in my ears, but never as loudly as they did on this day: *Tomorrow, and tomorrow, and tomorrow / Creeps in this petty pace from day to day / To the last syllable of recorded time.*

~

While my immediate colleagues treated me with cotton wool, there were dozens of strangers spread across four geographical locations in Australia with whom I needed to communicate. After several years working at the law firm my role had evolved. Now I was responsible for a national program of charitable activities that involved staff in all four offices. Mostly I enjoyed this job, which required a high level of telephone and email contact with people across our offices. But I didn't know who, if any of them, knew that I had just lost my husband. Talking to people I'd never met face to face, or reading an email from a colleague I barely knew, I would search their words for a veiled reference to my circumstances. I needed to know that other people understood I was not the same person I had been a few short weeks ago.

I didn't help myself in making any difference within me apparent to others. Weeks passed. As far as my colleagues and my own boss were concerned, there was no change in my professional demeanour. I turned up, read emails, organised meetings, *ran* meetings, and generally thought clearly enough to function. Deadlines were met, budgets were monitored, and my state-based committees faithfully implemented their respective programs that I oversaw. I wore makeup and dry-cleaned clothes. I *managed*.

The most difficult periods of each working day were lunch-time and the trip home. Food halls underneath office towers are depressing at the best of times, but watching people line up for their sandwich or deep-fried heart attack regularly reduced me to tears. I felt like an anthropologist who had returned from another planet, desperate to cut these strangers with the razor's edge of my misery.

'Don't you realise how meaningless it is to eat?! Don't you know that you will die — tonight, next year, in fifty years? That you are alive, and that you are squandering the fact that you still breathe? What are you doing with the time you have left?' I wandered around watching people eat junk, talk about nothing, waste time. Here was the jewellery store in which I had purchased the earrings I wore with my wedding dress. There was the cafe where I often met John while he was still working at his office in the city. I fantasised about the life I had lost at the same time as I looked with despair on my solitary new one. The clash of past and present created a feeling of intense pressure on my chest, as though I had to squeeze out each breath I took. I felt guilty for feeling hungry, so I would hastily buy a salad sandwich and scurry back upstairs to my office, shut the door, chew, swallow, cry. I wondered if other people's tears tasted the same as mine.

Colleagues asked me to make presentations or write reports, their tone suggesting that each task somehow had a point to it. Elegant sentences about nothing of consequence appeared on the computer screen in front of my eyes while tears edged down either side of my face. The office door stayed mostly shut. I was on automatic pilot: not mentally engaged in flying the plane, but somehow keeping it in the air.

It was so easy to focus intensely on work. Seductive, almost. I wasn't consciously trying to mask my grief. I caught myself staring at the screen after long blank minutes, my eyes blinking back tears, often enough to know that grief seeps through most mundane situations at one time or another. What was so charming about being back in the office environment was the easy fix available in the sense of administrative productivity. I could send an email, organise a presentation, write the annual report. To other people this indicated meaningful effort. Seeing something in the workplace change or happen as a result of my efforts, no matter how menial, was satisfying. In the continuum of satisfaction it was small potatoes, but for the time being it was all I could muster. It would have to do.

John and I loved the ritual of sharing a meal, and made almost daily use of the dining room. The room was the darkest in the house, on the south side we shared with our neighbours, and was home to our rapidly diminishing wine collection. We set the table, lit candles, and used a decanter. Admittedly we often ate pizza on our laps in front of the television when we were watching a movie — John was especially fond of classic westerns and was determined to show the sceptic in me the delights of films such as *How the West was Won* and *Once Upon a Time in the West* — but there was a sense of occasion to the way we ate dinner together at the table that made it the highlight of my day. Before he lost his mobility, John loved pottering in the kitchen, particularly on a Sunday night.

I experienced my first ever Yorkshire pudding at that dining table. The first time my parents came over for dinner, John roasted a duck. He wasn't afraid of experimenting.

On our first New Year's Eve together, we threw a dinner party for eight people. During the day we went to the harbourside fish market and talked to the fishmonger about how much cooking time on the barbecue our barramundi would take. The fish was massive, probably two inches thick around the middle, and needed cooking for twenty minutes on each side. It barely fit inside the kettle-top barbecue that lived on our back deck. We brought the fish to the dining room table — it was just big enough to accommodate our guests, the enormous fish on its serving platter, the vegetables, the bread, the sauces we'd made from scratch using herbs from our garden, and all our glassware and dishes. Instantly the room was transformed. Friends, loaves, wine and fish: the scene reminded me of one of those happy medieval banquets depicted in paintings.

Each afternoon I felt a surge of relief at another workday being over. But catching the bus home was one more labour to endure. My sunglasses shielded the other passengers from my wet eyes on the stop-start journey west. My stomach knotted with the agony of knowing that, as the sun set, the hardest part of my day was only just beginning.

Getting off the bus like all the other commuters who shared my stop, I stared blankly at the traffic crawling along the major thoroughfare. Waiting for the lights to change I concentrated on cultivating an attitude of studied indifference to my surroundings, which helped minimise the risk of bursting with sadness like a fire hydrant in the middle of peak-hour traffic. I dreaded the lights changing. A green walk signal was one less barrier to returning home.

Between the bus stop and my empty house a few minutes away, my pace was so slow, like an old-fashioned wind-up doll that was always threatening to come to a complete stop. I longed for someone to come up behind me and wind the key in my back to help me keep moving. I was exquisitely alert to the sound of my own breathing, and the physical act of moving through air thick with sadness and memory as I placed one deliberate foot after another on the footpath. I remember looking down at my lethargic feet, marvelling at how they knew how to function.

Once inside my front door I collapsed with a potent sensation of relief and felt the hot air escape my sad balloon. In front of me were long hours to fill with the mindless distraction of television, and the long night in which bed was literally the last of a few places I tried to find sleep. In the living room I watched multiple episodes of *Law and Order: Special Victims Unit*, finding its formulaic narrative structure soothing. Despite the show's often gruesome subject matter, there was more often than not resolution at the end of each episode. I knew what to expect. I wouldn't be taken by surprise. The central characters might sustain an injury, but they wouldn't die. I watched the paint crumble to the floorboards and left it there. It took too much energy to clean up the mess. There would be more of it in the morning anyway.

Spending time in the kitchen gave me something productive to do. I cooked and ate too much of the things that John had liked me to prepare — the baked salmon, the Thai-style chilli basil chicken, the pork and fennel sausages with a simple salad. Preparing these dishes had nothing to do with hunger; I just preferred spending time in the kitchen to anywhere else in the house.

I matched my wine to my food and drank like someone dying of thirst. Holding the wine glass gave me something to do with my hands, as playing the piano only made me weep. Briefly I considered taking up smoking. Time passed while I watched the wine diminish in my glass, then topped it up and sipped it down again. I tried convincing myself that the third or fourth glass of wine would help me sleep, but knew better. Sleep never came until after that inevitable moment, some time late every evening, when I suddenly began howling until I was exhausted from it. Only then would I fall asleep. At three or four in the morning I would wake up, the television on or a CD playing, and toss and turn for a minute while I remembered I was on the sofa. Still, I did not want to go to bed. My fervent desire was always to go back to sleep where I lay. Inevitably that did not happen and reluctantly I moved to my bed, where I would lie awake until just before the dawn. Just an hour or two before it was time to get up and go to work.

At unexpected moments I found myself overpowered by a wave of grief that swamped without warning. When I reached for a saucepan in its cluttered drawer; when I folded the sheets, washed and dried, to put them away; when I sat on the couch flicking through a magazine; sometimes while I stood in the hallway, keys still in my hand from letting myself in the front door. On occasion these waves of grief literally felled me: I dropped to the ground, slumped as if the puppet strings I had been relying on to hold me up had failed. One time my wailing was so energetic I propelled myself off the couch: my body couldn't contain the energy being expelled in grieving. Finally I understood the use of the word 'spent' to mean exhausted.

The wheels of my mind were spinning faster and faster but I was going nowhere, racing and totally bogged at the same time. As the months passed there was no escape from my own head. Wherever I went, I was there. And John was not. I had longed for routine, but never anticipated such an unhelpful one. I was caught in its thick mud.

—◌

About a month after I returned to work I decided it was an appropriate time to fly to my employer's Melbourne office. It was about eight weeks since John's death. I had arranged some meetings to justify the flight. After several weeks back on deck I had begun to feel very uncomfortable when I realised that stretches of time had passed — half an hour at my desk, for example, or the entire duration of a telephone conversation about something procedural and detail-oriented — in which I felt relatively 'normal'. In which I wasn't conscious of my widowhood. It was not right for me to feel anything like normal. I couldn't fathom how it was possible for me to function with accuracy and competence. I had never been so disgusted with how *capable* I was.

I didn't realise it at the time, but flying to Melbourne was the first in a series of experiments I conducted upon myself over the course of my first year as a widow. The productive relief I had found in the office was causing me anxiety on a different level. Ruthless efficiency was an unintended side-effect of my own prescription to return to work so quickly. Apparently I was 'doing well'. This phrase was bandied about by co-workers, neighbours, friends, and shopkeepers. It was intended as encouragement, but every time I heard it I felt guilty. Why couldn't they see my devastation? How could I talk and work and eat and laugh as if nothing had changed? My diagnosis demanded that I test myself. To titrate my own dose. While the rest of the world was oblivious to my efforts, I was trying to ascertain what kind of a widow I really was.

It didn't take long. After the usual early-morning queue for taxis outside Melbourne Airport, I sat down in the back seat, pulled out my mobile phone from my handbag, and dialled our home number. It wasn't until the phone started ringing that I realised what I'd done.

He's not there to answer the phone anymore. He's dead.

I always used to call John from inside the taxi to let him know I'd landed safely and to see how his morning was progressing: what sort of pain he was in, if he'd gone back to sleep after I left the house, whether the nurse had arrived yet to prepare his medication. I squeezed my eyes to try to stop the tears from coming, but I was too sad and my face crumpled. Instantly I was aware of how I had tricked myself into thinking everything was normal. The desire to talk to John again, to enjoy even the sort of quick domestic exchange many couples take for granted, was overwhelming. I was shocked by how naturally I had picked up the phone to call my husband. For a long moment I had forgotten he was dead, and suddenly was forced to know it again as if for the first time. The bliss of forgetting. The agony of remembering. None of this was normal. I propped my elbow on the inside window ledge so as to support my hand as it shielded my face from the taxidriver, and quietly sobbed all the way to the office.

13

When John showed me the website for the apartment in Noosa where we would be staying for five days with our friends Maria and Paul, who were visiting from London, my jaw dropped. From the apartment's enormous balcony, complete with a spa and a barbecue and enough outdoor seating for a small village, you could see all the way across the sparkling bay to the national park beyond.

'I checked with the hotel reception and made sure our apartment is accessible by elevator, so we can just get out of the car and go straight up,' he said. John was pleased to have been able to find the apartment online and make all our arrangements from his home office. The driver of a hard bargain, John had even secured us an impressive nightly rate, far lower than the price advertised on the hotel website. Our friends, who travel extensively, had never been to Queensland. John and I were so excited to be going on holiday with them. We needed a break.

In the three months since our wedding, John's pain had worsened considerably and his doctors were having trouble finding a suitable mix of medications to treat it. He had not been able to sleep more than forty-five minutes at a stretch, which made the nights long and the days short, as he spent the bulk of them dozing on the sofa, bathed in the sunlight that stole through the living room windows and revealed the decaying wood in the windowsills.

As a result he was not able to work a regular office schedule. For two nights we had even tried sleeping in separate beds — he in the guest room, me in our room, and then vice versa — to help him get a decent night's sleep. Whatever marginal improvement was achieved was offset by the fact that neither of us was satisfied with this arrangement. We agreed our bed was sacrosanct: there would be no sleeping in separate beds unless circumstances dictated that it was absolutely critical.

We consulted an orthopedic surgeon about a potential replacement of John's right femur, desperately hoping surgery would be able to give John the ability to walk again without crutches. Matter-of-factly the surgeon informed us that John's hip and pelvis were so ravaged by cancer that there was no existing bone strong enough to which he could reliably attach the hypothetical prosthetic bone. Orthopedic surgeons are not known as carpenters by their medical colleagues for nothing: even the best carpenter is only as good as the foundation into which he hammers a new piece of wood. That day I drove us home, despairing at another hope quashed, and frustrated at our diminishing options. John took most of these regular setbacks in his compromised stride, but even he baulked at opening the mail a few weeks later to find a speeding ticket with his name on it. By looking in my diary we traced the time and date of the fine to the drive home following that appointment. John wore the demerit points because the car was registered to him, even though he hadn't been able to drive it for months.

Since John was no longer able to drive, commuting to his office had become impossible, and he worked from home. The single impediment to his effectiveness was the level of pain he was in on any given day. If his pain was not managed then it obliterated everything else, making conversation and concentration impossible.

John now required a daily visit from a team of palliative care nurses. A nurse appeared on our doorstep each morning, much like the newspaper, but according to a schedule that to the last remained vague. These nurses, who even had a key to let themselves in if I wasn't home to answer the door, worked in mysterious ways. Their job was to monitor John's condition and to prepare the narcotic mixture that meted out pain relief via the most striking new addition to our married life: the syringe-driver. A small rectangular mechanism made of plastic in which the syringe full of multiple medications sat, the driver ensured a consistent delivery of medication over twelve or twenty-four hours (depending on the rate at which delivery was set). The medication found its way into John's bloodstream through a thin catheter attached at one end to the syringe, and at the other to a needle that stayed in one place — his upper arms and abdomen were the usual sites — for two days before the nurses changed the site to avoid infection.

Each nurse had a different personality, dress style, sense of humour. Some seemed to need a lot more room to work than others. Paradoxically, the physically largest nurse took up the least space: her preparation of the narcotic mix for John's syringe was tidy and self-contained. Other nurses liked to spread out and take their time, as if they were in their own kitchen preparing for a dinner party. We were always bemused that they usually prepared the narcotics in the dining room, where we kept the wine, our legal drug of choice. The dining room, on the other side of the central hallway from the living room, was the darkest and coolest room in the house. While the dining room might have been the best location for the wine bottles, a new collection — of glass vials and syringes and sterile swabs — was not quite what we imagined would start to appear on its central table.

With the syringe slotted into the driver the whole mechanism had the dimensions of a video cassette. John carried it around with him wherever he went, encased in a navy pouch with an elasticised strap that hung around his neck. He referred to it as his 'little navy handbag', but he didn't care what it looked like or that he had to wear it constantly. As long as it did the job of managing his pain it was welcome in our home. John wore it everywhere except the shower. In bed at night I fell asleep to the intermittent whirring sound the driver emitted each time it released a surge of medicine into John's bloodstream.

The second navy-coloured accessory the palliative care nurses provided John was a collapsible wheelchair with small wheels for trips that were too long for him to make using the crutches. He was relieved to have the collapsible chair to take to Noosa, even though someone else would have to push him.

We could not take with us the third item the nurses had recently lent us: a special mattress designed to reduce John's pain while lying in bed. John's doctors announced this unplanned addition to our interior décor at the end of John's ten-day stint in hospital in January, having experimented with pharmacological options for pain relief in their controlled environment. The mattress undulated gently every few minutes with a slowly rolling wave from one end to the other. It was powered by a pump that plugged into the nearest electrical socket. The purpose of the undulating mattress was to prevent pressure points and the accompanying risk of bedsores. The mattress was the size of a single bed, four or five inches thick, and encased in a thick blue vinyl. John and I concluded that royal blue must be the team colour of palliative care.

We covered the ungainly vinyl with a single-bed sheet, but nothing could disguise the fact that one half of our queen-sized marital bed was a lot higher than the other. Reclining in it together, we could no longer look at each other face to face. John was not only higher in the air than me due to the new mattress, he was also resting at an angle (rather than lying down) due to the intricate arrangement of cushions to help relieve the pressure on the primary tumour in his lower back. The cushions' bulk pushed him a considerable way down the bed, so that when I lay down my head was in line with the cushions rather than John's head. Instead of lying in my new husband's arms and staring into his eyes, I stared into a wall of blue instead. I couldn't even see John from where

I lay — he was a long way above me on his new mattress. When I wriggled into a new sleeping position, there was no body heat from John, just a cold unyielding vinyl. The undulating mechanism proved immediately beneficial and helped John to sleep, so it wasn't going anywhere. I hated that mattress.

———❧

The light-weight wheelchair collapsed as easily as a stroller, and we checked it in as oversize baggage on our flight to Queensland. Walking outside Maroochydore Airport into the blazing afternoon, the intense sunshine enveloped us like a blanket. The air shimmered in front of our eyes as we made our way to the hire car, and the asphalt beneath our feet radiated heat. Immediately this felt like, smelled like, a real holiday. It was glorious to be away with friends, to relax for a few days after the rollercoaster of medical trials and errors John had endured in the last few months.

After a half-hour drive we arrived at our holiday apartment. The building was situated proudly on the hillside closest to the national park at the south end of Hastings Street. A hillside that turned out to be on a sharp incline, with at least twenty-five metres of roadway to navigate between Hastings Street below us and the entry to the apartment building above. I should have realised that the website's unfettered view of our lush surrounds from the terrace of our apartment came at a literally steep price.

'How the hell are we going to get you up and down from here?' I said anxiously, as Paul steered the car into the building's car park. It was one thing to drive up the road and into the driveway, but another thing entirely for me to push John up the same slope. I could barely manoeuvre a shopping trolley in a straight line on a flat surface. Imagining John toppling out of the wheelchair on the way down the hill, or stuck fast at the bottom as I tried to push him up it, I couldn't help but see the short steep incline as a symbol of all our uphill battles.

John dismissed my concern with a wave of his hand. 'That's why Paul's here,' he said, chuckling. Paul's large build and easygoing disposition made light work of the job. And, once we were safely at the bottom of the hill, Noosa was highly accessible — it's largely flat and well designed with plenty of ramps. Over the course of five days we confirmed the accessibility of several wine bars, restaurants, and boardwalk cafes, and were able to stumble home as easily as we had arrived. Friends from Brisbane drove the one and a half hours north to join us for a weekend, and the six of us enjoyed a long and liquid dinner. I was struck by the sheer luxury of this social ritual. Laughing and relaxing together. It was all so normal. So *healthy*.

~

Less so was the knock on our apartment door the next morning.

'That must be my drug dealer,' John announced to our surprised friends as I moved towards the door. Sure enough, when

I opened it, there was a local nurse bearing narcotic gifts. We had arranged through the palliative care service for a nurse to meet us at the apartment with the medication for John's syringe-driver, as we could only take with us from Sydney a certain volume of some of his restricted drugs. John's drug-dealing joke would have been funnier if some of the supplies she brought did not have a street value. One of our favourite ways to surprise friends was to show them the enormous glass ampoules — thick as thumbs — of Ketamine, a horse tranquilliser known colloquially as 'Special K'. Maria's eyes nearly popped when she saw the size of the glass vial and the mass of equipment needed to formulate the liquid supply for the syringe-driver. John and I never saw the cumulative power of the drug paraphernalia and vials and tubes and needles and assorted medical equipment — they were simply the means to attain our common goal of minimising his pain and helping us to live each day, as best we could, according to our mantra.

As normal as possible, for as long as possible.

~

When you cannot bear any weight on your legs, it takes some creativity to continue a sex life. Ours all but ended around the time of our wedding. Many comedians joke about how there's less sex after marriage. Well, we had no sex at all, but it wasn't for lack of desire. It was simply no longer physically possible. Imagine any position: it was out of the question. John's extreme physical pain obliterated all other sensations and distracted him from his naturally frisky tendencies. For me, on the other hand, a picture of health and in love with my husband, it was a severe and distressing loss that I had to mourn while John was still alive. Here was this man I had found at last, the person I loved and trusted most in the world. I wanted to hold him close, to rub my hands up and down and over and under him, to wrap myself around him, to feel him inside me. We couldn't enjoy any of these things anymore because they caused John intense pain. We were limited to hugs and gentle kisses and holding hands. He just had so much pain, or was drowsy or vague because of his drugs, that he often didn't notice or couldn't respond to my need for physical affection. But we tried our best. Over time we devised a method of hugging in which I knelt on the ground, facing John sitting in a chair, but with me at an angle such that I could reach across his shoulders with one arm and across his chest with the other. He could then in turn grasp me so that his arms reached almost around my waist without having to twist his lower back. We always had to be gentle, but we kissed each other on the lips, on our cheeks, our eyes, our necks, our hands. We held each other, still, but charged with energy like a butterfly whose wings vibrate so fast they are invisible to the naked eye.

~

There were so many aspects of John's and my life together that we did not choose. I often longed to experience one day, or a whole week when I was feeling greedy, in which we could spend time together without our ever-present third wheel. I wondered what it would be like for us just to *be*, unconstrained by the demands of regular medication, nurses' visits, doctors' appointments, and John's omnipresent pain.

Tough moments were part and parcel of our life, but they were far from common. We did not live as if we were constantly riding a rollercoaster, as I think some of my immediate family and work colleagues pictured it. We did not race upwards to a brief peak — some perfect moment in which there was no pain, no cancer, no shadow of death — and then descend with terrifying speed to the depths of despair, spending the in-between times in limbo, waiting for the next spike up or down. On the contrary, John and I spent most of our time together talking and laughing. We had our routines and rituals like any couple. We watched films and entertained friends, and whiled away many hours on the back deck reading, eating and drinking, enjoying our patch of garden. One of the many double-edged gifts of this period of my life was losing the otherwise natural human tendency to take each other for granted. It was impossible, given the circumstances of our relationship, to forget how miraculous it was that we met; that were it not for our previous failed relationships, neither of us would have met the mutual friends who eventually brought us together; that we did not know how much time was ours to share, so naturally it was not to be wasted. As a couple we simply vaulted over the low-level irritations and petty squabbles that would inevitably have been ours to experience and chafe against in any 'healthy' relationship.

'Not many people are as lucky as you and me,' John often said, with quiet conviction. We clutched each other as hard as we dared and cherished these small moments. They contained the whole world we had made together. John's physical pain sharpened our mutual understanding, honed our perception of what was valuable, even though it dulled his senses and together we felt that loss in other, more literal, ways. As a couple the peculiar benefit of the constraints of John's disease was, to paraphrase William Blake, to be able to see our world in these grains of sand; an eternity in each of these fleeting moments.

~

On our last day in Noosa John wore the sandals he had bought the previous day after an exhaustive search for a pair of summer shoes that could accommodate his feet, which were beginning to swell due to immobility and poor circulation. The sun shone down relentlessly as Paul, Maria, John, and I strolled the boardwalk along Main Beach, taking photos and gawping at a pod of dolphins frolicking close to the shore. I noticed my freckled arms had taken on a tinge of pink, but never thought of the sun's power over John's newly exposed and ghost-pale feet.

~

The relaxation benefits of our holiday lasted less than twenty-four hours. I went into the office, while our friends took John out in our neighbourhood. John wrote about this day in one of his 'Cancer Boy Updates':

> On returning to Sydney, Paul, Maria and myself went for a coffee through Leichhardt, which I have previously described as 'Little Italy'. I was in my wheelchair and decided to move into a 'proper chair' in the cafe. Whilst doing this, I heard a loud crack from my leg, which was soon joined by a mind-jarring amount of pain. I had broken the top of my femur!

John's retrospective narratives of pain, with their slightly old-fashioned grammar and excited exclamation points, read like a *Boy's Own* adventure. With a broken bone, John was now in too much pain to lie down at all, so he had to sit on the couch, day and night. His legs swelled up quickly to twice their previous size as a result of being constantly in that sitting position. The top of John's right foot had been quite burnt by exposure through his sandals to the intense Noosa sunshine. This was not a problem until the fluid from his swelling legs decided to spread to his feet, and then, to our horror, to escape through the site of the tender sunburnt skin. The resulting sore, which looked as though John's right foot had erupted in a combination of pus, blood, and unidentifiable fluid, was unspeakable to behold.

If the introduction of John's syringe-driver occasioned a marked increase in the amount of medication in our house, then his brand-new infected right foot caused an immediate doubling of the amount of equipment required for the nurses to attend to it. The syringes in three different sizes, the alcohol swabs, and the boxes of morphine and horse tranquilliser had already set up camp in our dining room. With the new disaster as ammunition, the nurses began colonising more of the house: bandages, gauze, scissors, tape, wound dressings and other things I could never quite identify now took up residence on the coffee table in our living room, the mantelpiece above the fireplace, and on our bedside tables. Like nature, the nurses abhorred a vacuum.

John accepted without complaint the multiple invasions of personal and physical space that his medical care represented. After so many years of fighting the disease, he had grown accustomed to it. He simply saw the nurses for what and who they were: trained professionals there to help him. A succession of qualified strangers assisted John to undress, dry him after his shower, check his catheter, then dress him. John somehow maintained his dignity in the most undignified of circumstances — somebody was always touching him, poking and prodding with needles and syringes full of medication, inspecting parts of his body, observing his pain.

I admired the nurses and professional care-givers, because

there was no way I could have done this work for anyone else but John. For me this was a labour of love, though I didn't always love the labour.

John's method of dealing with the constant invasion of his privacy was humour and curiosity: he liked joking around with the nurses, and finding out about the lives his care-givers led outside of his appointment with them. He even tried coaching a Greek carer with her grammar, although I was never sure if she had invited his well-intended instruction.

After they left the house he would often share his more acerbic comments with me. 'I wish she would change her clothes,' he said of one care-giver who helped him shower and dress on Tuesday mornings. 'Every week she wears the same thing — and she *reeks* of smoke. It's absolutely disgusting.'

~

In contrast to John's grace and dignity in the face of all he had to endure, my response to the invasion of our home was much more controlling. I reached my limit the day I knelt down to open one of the bathroom cupboards to find all manner of plastic-sealed equipment spilling out. I flopped on the cold terracotta tiles and burst into tears. The damp rising through the walls might have been beyond my control, but there was no way these nurses were going to commandeer our bathroom. Decrepit as its ceiling was, this room was the one remaining oasis in the house for stolen minutes of relaxation. The rest of the house, our bedroom included, might incrementally be conceding its privacy, but not this room. Not yet.

A few weeks passed before I found a solution while out grocery shopping. Along with bags of meat and vegetables, I lugged home a five-drawer trolley on caster wheels. John just shook his head at me and chuckled as I promptly organised all the wayward items into its translucent sliding drawers, and wheeled the trolley into the dining room next to the table where the nurses sat to prepare his narcotic mix. He understood I needed to at least try to assert some control. I couldn't stop the spread of disease through his body, but I could do something about the progress of medical equipment through our home. The nurses were mightily impressed with my organisational skills. They could now find anything they needed within arm's reach, and they even had extra room to put new items they might bring with them. John's medication was all in the one place. And I had my bathroom back.

~

Living from day to day as we did, noticing an improvement in the infected sore was a cause for celebration and renewed hope. Somehow the global issue of John's terminal illness could be not ignored, but disguised by attending to his diverse local complications. In this way John and I forged ahead with daily life, confronting progress and setbacks each week. Looking at our situation from the outside, it would make sense to wonder why, for example, I did not stop working.

There were many reasons. To begin with, I had a very understanding employer with the necessary resources to enable me to work from home or out of the office as circumstances required. John had regular appointments with specialists to which I took him; on those days I worked from home. I had access to the help of an administrative assistant who kept a lot of the minutiae under control with processes we had already implemented, and I conducted most of my work by email and telephone. A monthly interstate trip to meet colleagues face to face was valuable because it allowed me to remain visible while also being off their short-term radar in between meetings, as long as I followed through on what I said I was going to do. I suspect that continuing to work in a job that had seniority and influence gave me some level of psychological comfort. I couldn't always be sanguine at four o'clock in the morning administering John's second breakthrough dose of morphine in one night, but I could manage a six-figure budget.

Most important, my continuing to work provided John and me with some semblance of a normal life. I kept juggling the increasing number of balls that life threw at us, and focused on each day. The big picture wasn't of any help in our situation. On the several occasions when I asked John if he thought I should stop working, he always said no, not yet. 'We'll know when the time comes,' he said.

Before I left for work on the days I went into the office, I selected his clothes and laid them on the edge of the bed for the nurse or professional care-giver (depending on what day of the week it was). I prepared John's lunch, ensured he had the requisite items to make several of his beloved cups of tea, and put them into a squat bar-fridge that my father had found somewhere. It was the ugliest shade of poo-brown we'd ever seen, but it worked and was within John's physical reach, and it was free. John went back to sleep immediately after I kissed him goodbye, then woke to the sound of the nurse entering the house a couple of hours later. I usually called him from work at around twelve-thirty, when he was just starting his day, to check in. A few times a week he had visitors — colleagues from his office, old friends, my father — who brought him lunch to share. Then he read and slept his way through the rest of the afternoon until I arrived home between five and six o'clock.

I tried to remember everything he needed, but I was only human. One time I was out of the office at a meeting when John rang to lodge a complaint in his own inimitable fashion. I still have his voicemail message:

Wifey! Where are you? I went to . . . to the fridge to get me lunch and . . . and . . . there was nothing there! (Mock sob.) The cupboard was bare! Poor Johnny. Call him now. He misses you. (Mock sob.)

The problem was that we really believed we would know when the time was right for me to stop working. We were wrong. John's final decline was so sharp, we were shocked that even the time we had planned to share when I took extended leave was snatched away from us. I felt cheated, like a pregnant woman who takes maternity leave early in order to prepare for her baby's arrival, but gives birth weeks earlier than predicted. Only in our case it wasn't an unplanned arrival, but a departure.

~

My best efforts to keep John's medicine and bandages tidy were doing little to improve the actual infected sore on his foot. It was soon evident there was no choice but for John to be hospitalised to treat it. The results were immediate, and confidently I wrote to a friend:

> I'm pleased to report the swelling has subsided, the sore on his foot has almost healed, and he is now working with a physiotherapist to get him back on his relatively 'good' left leg so that he can continue using crutches to get around for a while longer, at least at home.

For a couple of educated and articulate white-collar types, the extent of our mutual delusion was profound. John and I had hoped that somehow, with physiotherapy or the right medication, he might be able to go back to using his walking stick, maybe even drive his car again. That our optimism would triumph over all evidence to the contrary. To our mutual dismay, John walked into hospital using crutches, but it was for the last time. He would never stand upright again.

14

In January 2005, three months after John died, I asked a male friend to accompany me to a concert at the Opera House as part of the annual Sydney Festival. Several months earlier I had purchased two tickets to see Philip Glass and his ensemble perform the music of one of his film scores, while the film was screened above the musicians in the Concert Hall. Buying the tickets so far in advance had been a desperate tactic I hoped could ensure that John and I would see the concert together. Now, although John was no longer alive, his absence would form no basis for a refund. The show would go on without him.

I knew the music would nourish me, but I didn't feel up to going to such a public venue by myself. Public or private, there weren't many places I specifically wanted to go. In the middle of summer I hadn't once gone for a swim or to the beach. At the time there was sufficient water still inside my house, and the sunshine was welcome mainly because it would help the bricks to dry. Neither had I been to the cinema or my local jazz club. Both were in walking distance, but I simply couldn't be bothered. I stayed at home, watching films, reading home-improvement magazines, entertaining the close friends who liked to check in to see I was all right. Sometimes I joined a friend for dinner at a local restaurant, but I preferred it when my friends and family stopped by the house.

I could set the table on the back deck for lunch or dinner just like I used to do with John. I loved having someone to cook for. The deck looked out on the garden, secluded and quiet. Just past the clothesline the lemon tree flourished, producing so much fruit I could regularly give a bagful to my neighbour, another to my parents, and have plenty left over. The rosemary bush next to it thrived as well, the star performer in my fledgling herb garden. Life, however circumscribed, was evident in this garden, and the deck was a safe place for me to observe it.

There's a very small handful of unattached people I know who would want to see Philip Glass in concert, and Peter was one of them. My sodden brain slowly turned over a series of thoughts like the letters on an airport destination board trying to settle on their next configuration: going out to a concert seemed so decadent, but it would be a waste of money not to make use of the tickets. Attending a public performance with a man who was not my husband felt inappropriate. While others might not throw stones at me, I would have to dodge my own slings and arrows. Getting out of the house for an evening was probably a good idea, but I would have to get dressed up. John would want me to go. That last one seemed to do the trick. Peter kindly agreed to come with me when I asked him. He had recently gone through a divorce, so we were like two birds with broken wings.

Inevitably we ran into married friends of mine in the foyer of the Concert Hall. They were attending the same concert as we were. I was delighted to see them, and made the necessary introductions.

'Virginia! You look great!' Andrea exclaimed, beaming at me, her eyes wide.

'Oh! I do? Um . . . thank you,' I stammered, not knowing how to play her unexpected curve-ball. *Great*? I choked on the word as if it were gristle lodged in my throat. I thought Andrea and Tom knew me well. They were at my wedding. They *know*. They seemed to be judging my state of mind based on whether or not I was wearing lipstick. On my ability to put an outfit together. *Great* was a strong word to use, in the circumstances. At least, it felt that way to me. Certainly Andrea didn't choose her words as carefully as I listened to them. She surreptitiously gave Peter the once-over. I was shocked to realise she was wondering if he and I were *dating*. If we might be *having sex*. As attractive as Peter was, the thought of any man touching me was as unwelcome as my new life. I felt guilty for days afterwards. For being healthy, for being able to attend the concert — and to enjoy it — for leaving the house, and relaxing in the company of a man I knew and trusted. For looking, as far as the rest of the world could determine, that my life had not capsized.

~

A pattern of well-intended yet misplaced compliments became a recurring motif of my early widowhood. Outwardly I looked much the same, I suppose, although my hair, inevitably, had become shorter than it was in the months before John's death, when there was no time to get to the hairdresser. A few weeks after John's funeral I went to see Orlando, the only straight male hairdresser in Sydney, and asked him to cut it short. Short on top, short at the nape of my neck, short at the sides. I wanted to be shorn like a sheep. Nothing soft, nothing sensuous. Nothing that would draw attention to my face, my figure, my existence. Looking with new eyes at a photograph from that time, I'm surprised how well I succeeded. My spiky razor-savaged haircut screamed at the world, as I could not: *I wish my hair would stop growing. I wish that I would stop breathing. Do not look at me. I am not to be looked at. I am alone. I want to be left alone.*

At home in front of the mirror I desperately sought out physical signs — new wrinkles, a grey hair, or a tooth suddenly coming loose — as evidence of my grief. I searched in vain for something about my appearance I could point to that marked me as *other*, that identified me as someone around whom it would be appreciated if you trod carefully. To my dismay, I had even managed to find again much of the weight I had lost during John's final months, which only gave me something else to feel guilty about.

'You gannet! I can't believe how much you can eat,' John had often said to me, part tease, part admiration. My natural curves tend to accommodate a waxing waistline, although I didn't complain when I started to lose the 'happy kilos' I had packed on in our first year together. So feeling hungry now, as a widow, was confusing.

Shouldn't I be a physical shadow of my former self? I longed for a black armband to differentiate mine from the countless variations of melancholy on other people's faces. To prove to them, and to myself, that I really did grieve every day, whether you could see it or not. I almost envied Hawthorne's Hester Prynne her scarlet letter — although I would have preferred mine to have been an elegant black W.

As time goes on I am regularly told that I look younger than my years. But I feel older than most people I know.

15

I entered hospital on crutches and left in a wheelchair. Basically, my legs had both become non-weight bearing. The disease is slowly getting the better of my mobility.

A week after leaving hospital a monumental occurrence took place — my brother David arrived from England. He could not have come at a more crucial time! That week had been one of the scariest of my life. It's hard to imagine when you are able bodied, just what it means to lose the use of one's legs. One needs assistance for damned near every task that one does, dressing, reaching tall things and reaching things on the floor. I need to use a special wheelchair just to use the toilet. Not only that, I need assistance to undress and dress as well. Virginia and myself had battled through this week with as much humour and understanding as we could muster but we were at our wits' end. David had never been such a ray of sunshine!

With David's help, we started to work out routines. Since he is considerably bigger and stronger than Virginia, we could make mistakes, like dropping me or me losing my balance, which David could save, with little pain to himself... and loads to me! It seemed like he had landed in heaven, where it was payback time for all those years when I was a nasty little shit of an older brother. We did however learn the best (least painful) way of undressing and dressing for a shower. How to get into and out of bed from the wheelchair. How to get into and out of the car from the wheelchair. All simple tasks before, but now torturous nightmares!

It was not all hard work for David's trip as we managed to do some of the tourist things that one must in Sydney — but not the Harbour Bridge walk! We ate and drank like kings both at home and in some of Sydney's wonderful restaurants. It was very sad to see him leave.

The appearance of John's brother from Cambridge just after Easter really did feel like a miracle. John had been using the wheelchair for about five days when David arrived to stay for two weeks. That first week with the chair was one of our toughest. John was grappling with the fact that now he needed my help to do most things, rather than just some things. From picking up something he had dropped on the floor, to selecting a bottle of wine from the rack we kept them in, to helping him dress and undress, he now relied on me completely.

During the three or four months to this moment, when John was using crutches, watching him teeter precariously while negotiating the single step down from the living room to the rear of the house was nerve-wracking enough. The difference now was that we were equally responsible for moving him safely around the house — and the house was not built for a wheelchair user. Immediately we saw the house from a new perspective. Steps were everywhere we looked. The two-inch-high tiled ceramic step that kept our shower water from travelling outside the shower recess now kept John from entering the shower at all. He could not access the kitchen either, because the fixed island workbench in the middle of the room obstructed the passage of his wheelchair. Even with the crutches the kitchen had been tricky — it was difficult and dangerous for John to open the fridge, for example, and hand me something from within it — but at least we had been able to continue sharing the room. We had kept a fold-up chair handy so John could sit on it and stir the contents of a saucepan, or chop some vegetables, or just talk to me while I prepared dinner. Now he was excluded from the hub of the house. The wheelchair transformed our relationship to our domestic space and made John a stranger inside his own home.

'What did I do to deserve this?' John shouted at one point, tears of frustration finally getting the better of him after several days trying to adapt to the wheelchair. 'Look at me! I'm such a fucking cripple!

'And it's not only me,' he cried. 'Look what I'm doing to you. You have to do everything for me.' He shook his head fiercely, trying to dispel some of his disappointment and rage.

I tried to comfort John as best I could, but knew that ultimately I could change nothing. I marvelled that of all possible things for him to despair over, the one that brought him to tears was the effect his immobility had on me.

My resistance to the wheelchair was more symbolic than tactical. Intellectually I was comfortable with the advent of the wheelchair: it made daily life easier and safer for John and, by extension, for me. What disturbed me was that the wheelchair represented tangible evidence that John was declining more rapidly than either of us had imagined. That the horizon was arriving much faster than we had anticipated. I often caught my breath at the gross unfairness of it, and at the indifference of fate. And yet we had no choice but to cope, to improvise, to make do. We were forced to live in two equally real, co-existent worlds at once: the world of our sheer joy of being with each other, being in love, and being newlywed; the other, the world in which we had to adapt constantly to a series of major changes, all of which were exerting an inexorable gravitational pull to John's death.

A handyman from the local council's home modification service — usually the province of elderly people with mobility impairments — removed the tiled step that to now had separated the shower recess from the floor of the bathroom. This small modification meant that John could be wheeled into and out of the shower without effort.

With David's help and a few weeks of trial and error, John and I refined a logical if complex routine for manoeuvring him safely around the house. The fact that John still had reasonable upper-body strength helped enormously, as he could support himself using his arms as I focused on lifting his legs to transfer him from his high-rise blue mattress into the commode, the ghastly-named waterproof counterpart to the wheelchair, which John used every morning for taking a shower and using the toilet. The commode featured a white vinyl cushioned seat with a strategically placed hole in its centre, and thick white plastic straps secured to a chrome frame at its back. The worst moments were when we were in mid-transfer, John entrusting his physical safety to me, and I realised I had forgotten some small but significant step in the process. Often it was forgetting to remove one or the other of the commode's removable footrests, or neglecting to lock the commode in place. Every minor slip I felt as a major failing. The short journey from bedroom to toilet was full of uneven heights, and every jolt coursed through John's ravaged body, so these obstacles were a test of John's trust, and a test of the driver's patience.

After the shower either the nurse or I towel-dried his back, his lower legs and feet, and returned to the bedroom, where we transferred John from the commode back to the bed to finish drying him and then to dress him. There is just no way to get a pair of trousers on a person whose legs won't hold him up other than for that person to be lying down. His feet were too swollen for socks, and as he had lost sensitivity in his feet he did not feel their absence despite the winter cold. With his trousers and shirt in place, we transferred John one more time, from the bed into the wheelchair. Once in the wheelchair we made sure the syringe-driver was connected and slung in its navy pouch around his neck, attached the chrome footrests for his puffed-up feet, and ensured the cushions underneath and behind him were arranged for maximum comfort. After two hours, he was finally ready for the day ahead.

If John had not experienced the cancer pain and nerve pain, the tasks of getting him in and out of bed, to and from the wheelchair, the toilet, the shower, dressing and undressing him would all have been straightforward. A lot to learn, a steep curve of new experiences and skills to acquire, but straightforward nonetheless. These tasks stood right on the border of technical skill and patience. I knew I had the patience; the technical skill was simply a matter of practice. Unfortunately, with each trial and every single error producing agonising pain in my husband, I was soon at my wits' end. He was relying on me and I felt I was failing him. I found it difficult to accept that I simply couldn't figure out ways to perform these simple tasks for John that didn't cause him paroxysms of pain. I realised that pain, rather than the wheelchair itself, was our relentless enemy.

'No one wheels me in and out of here like you do,' John told me one day after a smooth journey in the commode to the bathroom. The compliment made me feel as proud as if I had been awarded a Nobel Prize.

My father jumped at the chance to do something practical for us. His sense of helplessness in the face of John's tumours and his own robust health at the age of seventy meant he was primed to assist us given the slightest opportunity. A former builder and inveterate inventor, he came over straight away with his tape measure and a concerned frown. Mum accompanied him, bringing flowers and chocolate biscuits. The major discovery on this day was that the respective steps into each room at the back of the house were of slightly different heights. That meant our original dream of a false floor covering the entire back half of our house was not practicable. We decided the priority was to connect the bathroom and separate toilet with the false floor — the latter, thankfully, had almost a full turning-circle of room for John — and to move the study to a smaller spare room opposite the bathroom that had been piling up with the detritus of the house. That room happened to share the same height of entry step as the bathroom and toilet, making Dad's job slightly easier.

The next step was to procure the wood with which to construct the false floor, and the ramp that would lead at a gentle gradient from the false floor to the rest of the back of the house, providing John with easy access to the deck.

'You only want a bit of plywood, don't you?' Dad said. To him it was simply a quick point of clarification before heading off to his supplier.

'What do you mean?' I said.

'Well, it's only a temporary thing, isn't it?'

'It's not temporary for John, Dad,' I said quickly, diverting my tears with an overly sharp tone of voice. Never before had I appreciated the unconscious arrogance of the able-bodied. Suddenly John and I were members of a different community — disability — that any one of us can join, at any time. 'It's permanent for him, you know.' A set of two metal ramps, one for each side of the wheelchair, had constituted our interim solution for moving John about the house. They had accompanied us home from the hospital. The false wooden floor and ramp to the back of the house would have no whiff of interim about it. I was indignant.

'Oh, well, yes, I mean, yeah. Right. I just thought . . .' Dad had only been thinking about the expense of purchasing the sort of timber that would match our floorboards. But the costs weren't about the price of wood.

'I want the ramp to look as if it has always been there,' I said. 'It has to look like it's part of our home. I don't care how much the wood costs.' I was terrified.

The purpose of the new floor and ramp was to facilitate living, not simply to endure John's mobility impairment until such time as my father would dismantle them. The wooden boards needed to be an organic element of the house, incorporated into its ongoing life. Their appearance would not be an aberration or an eyesore.

My father set to work procuring the appropriate materials. He was fortunate to locate a parcel of karri wood in the quantity we required. A hardwood from the south-east corner of Western Australia, karri was formerly logged from old-growth forests, and these days is only available second-hand. I was thrilled when I discovered that karri was known for its durability, as if its long-lasting properties would somehow have a halo effect on John's longevity.

Dad carefully took measurements before installing the false floor and the ramp that led down from it to the original floor at a safe gradient. Our friends and the visiting nurses all agreed that he had managed to make a major modification to our home as unobtrusive as possible. John had the joy of movement around most of his own home. With the new floor and ramp in place, John could still come outside on to the deck. With some new extra-long tongs, he could still perform his duties at the barbecue. Friends could still come over and share a meal.

As normal as possible, for as long as possible.

Dad gave us our house back, and in the most dignified possible way. After a week or so of using the ramp, we could no longer imagine the house without it. The prospect of having to live elsewhere had been a real but unimaginable threat; now we didn't have to contemplate it. We could live our life, on our terms, in our own home.

~

But the wheelchair pushed our bedroom door wide open, and there was no way of ever closing it fully again. Over and above the parade of nursing staff, there wasn't much physical space left after the wheelchair and commode entered our lives and our bedroom. One day a palliative care nurse walked into our bedroom just as I started screaming, literally, at the top of my lungs, at the sight of the serious bedsore that one of Sydney's major public hospitals had allowed to develop on John's lower right leg while he was in their 'care' for one night a few weeks earlier. In all the hours he spent in one of their beds, no member of the nursing staff had moved him. The hideous bedsore was the inevitable result. That was the one occasion I had not taken John to hospital: instead I had flown to Melbourne for a series of meetings the day he was scheduled for another MRI scan. Because his primary tumour continued to grow and expand — now it was the size of a discus embedded in his lower back — it was physically impossible for John to lie down on it, as any pressure on the tumour caused agonising pain. For John to have an MRI scan he had to be hospitalised and go under general anesthetic: unconscious was the only way that he could possibly lie down as the scan required.

John had insisted I stay overnight in Melbourne rather than rush back the same day so I could visit him in hospital.

'I'll be all right, Pumpkin,' he said. 'You need a break from running around after me all the time.'

You need a break. Jesus.

John could neither see nor feel the pressure sore I screamed at. I screamed at the ugliness of the angry, infected wound; at the gross unfairness of John's having to deal with one more medical complication; at my guilt at not having been there with him, and my total inability to have prevented this from happening or now to make it go away. Looking at his swollen legs, I screamed at the fact that he couldn't wear the shoes I'd bought for him on our honeymoon — or any shoes now at all — as an emblem of all the losses we had to grieve together. I screamed at the realisation that John's body was no longer healthy enough to fight the bedsore. I screamed as I understood, finally, that his wound would never heal.

———෨

While we shed tears of frustration, alone and together, at the new intrusion into our married life the wheelchair represented; and while we did acknowledge, however reluctantly, its signalling of the final stages of John's disease; the coming of the wheelchair was far from bad news. It allowed us to get out of the house again. This was hugely liberating for John, who had been cooped up either at home or in a hospital bed for most of the previous two months. Best of all, being able to go out together again gave me hope that while the horizon was closer than we hoped, the parameters of our visible world had not shrunk too far, too soon.

So going to the coffee shop became an epic adventure. While our nearest cafe might have been a short distance as the crow flies, we had to navigate multiple obstacles that neither of us had ever noticed before. For example, before we even left the house I first had to move the car out of the driveway and park it on the street, because the driveway was the only way to get John from the house to the street (the brick path to the front door had two steps). The streetlight posts intruded on the footpath, leaving insufficient space to manoeuvre the wheelchair, so I had to push him along on the road. In order to get him on to the street, there was a short but steep dip between the edge of our kerb and the street proper, which meant I had to reverse John into the street otherwise I would risk tipping him out of the chair. We often joked that I should wear an 'L' permit on my back to indicate my learner's status in trying to push John. Cars inevitably drove by as we rattled slowly along the bitumen, which had never seemed bumpy before now. Drivers always took care to keep a wide berth, but we felt suddenly vulnerable having to utilise the road in this way. There was no choice but to proceed at a crawl, because every bump we travelled over coursed through John's nervous system like he was a voodoo doll covered in pins.

Once we had successfully navigated our own street, we had then to traverse a small car park, snake around a short connecting laneway and cross a busier road to arrive safely at the cafe. No sooner had we found the safest route than we had to learn to anticipate and counteract new and changing obstacles — a truck hurtling towards us, too wide for the laneway; a delivery of goods for one of the local shops taking up one of the rare sections of navigable footpath;

two friends, deep in conversation, not looking where they were going and nearly ploughing into us. Sometimes it felt like a Herculean task just to get this short distance. But the happiness on John's face as he chatted with the locals, our sense of achievement as we sipped our coffee and felt the sun on our backs and shared the Saturday newspaper together, was worth the precarious journey every time.

The supermarket became an exciting destination in itself, and getting there a thrilling goal. We did the shopping together as much as possible, searching for a wheelchair-accessible parking spot — often in vain — before taking the goods lift up to the supermarket entrance. Because the supermarket was flat, John pushed himself around the aisles and took charge of the list I had inevitably made. Sometimes we'd go our separate ways, each to get a few different things, and meet up again a few aisles further along. One time when we had split up, I glanced down one aisle to spot him whiz by at the opposite end. He was busy pushing the chair with both hands, and peering out over the top of an enormous box of Coco-Pops that he had wedged between his chin and his lap.

'They were on special,' he said later, not able to understand why I was laughing so much.

'Oh, darling boy,' I began as I leaned down to kiss him, but John cut me off.

'Don't tell me I look cute,' he said. 'I've told you a thousand times, I'm *not* cute.'

On one occasion, after several tours of the car park, we took a non-accessible spot out of desperation and did our best to get John comfortably in and out of the car. We had noticed a shiny new four-wheel drive parked in the most coveted accessible space and felt the usual pang of envy.

On our return, I unloaded the contents of our shopping trolley into the car's rear seat as John waited. Unbeknown to me, John had been watching the owners of the four-wheel drive return to their vehicle. Neither the driver nor his passenger used a wheelchair or exhibited any visible mobility impairment. They were simply a carefree young couple who felt no compunction whatsoever in taking a wheelchair parking spot. Sitting in the vehicle, ready to reverse out, they didn't see him coming.

John tapped on the driver's door. Even from where I stood I could see the driver's double-take as he looked down from his lofty height to see John in his chair, piercing him with those baby-blue eyes.

'Thanks very much, mate,' John said. 'Don't bloody well do it again.'

~

One night over dinner during his visit, John's brother had compared life with the wheelchair to the experience of smoking a cigar. 'It forces you to slow down,' David said, swirling an aged Barossa shiraz around a large glass, 'so it forces everything else to slow down as well.' He was right: time was concertinaing, slowing down and speeding up at once, compressing as we approached the end. His analogy was particularly helpful, especially to a woman who's always been in a hurry. But the end would arrive in the form of a steep decline, and we were accelerating without a clue as to when to expect it.

16

I started spending time again at a cafe, a few blocks from home, at which John and I had been a weekly fixture. Returning there had proven more difficult than going back to work. Although I had resumed office life too soon, the generic layout and depersonalised routines of the workplace provided a haven in which I could safely lose myself. There I could dress up in my corporate costume, talk in the vocabulary of my employer — using words and phrases that were meaningless in any other context such as, 'Do you have capacity?' and 'Let's take this discussion offline' — and daily play the part to which my name was professionally attached. Outside the make-believe of corporate life, in the real world of supermarkets and bookshops and petrol stations and cafes, I had no costume to wear, no official language in which to speak. The roles I used to play — wife, lover, best friend, companion, care-giver — were no longer available to me. I was an unemployed actor desperate for work.

At the cafe I sat in the same chair I used to sit in opposite John, ordered my coffee, and looked around at the waiters and other patrons. My solitude radiated from me like the sun. I wondered if anyone else noticed that John wasn't with me. As he had grown increasingly frail and thin, I had the impression that we became more noticeable as a couple in our neighbourhood. But no one else seemed to notice John's absence from this tableau, even though his face was all I saw as I sipped my cappuccino. The sense of his absence came and went like the tide, and usually bore little relationship to what I was doing at any given moment. One day I would be sitting at the cafe, wondering about little other than what I'd left off my grocery shopping list. The next week I would find tears collecting in my sunglasses, prompted by a sudden memory of how much he loved listening to The Police, or the way he took forever to brush his teeth. Sometimes John's death felt like it happened yesterday, or that it hadn't happened yet but was just about to. At other times he was simply away somewhere and I was waiting for him to come back so our life could resume.

I was waiting for my life to return to normal. But I was no longer the same person, and it began to dawn on me that there was no going back. The home I had to return to was not the one I wanted. Normal would take some time to define itself. To the outside world, perhaps I looked the same, but I knew I was changed forever. It wasn't just the feeling of literally having sat at this particular cafe or having looked out at the same streetscape from over the rim of my coffee cup before John became part of my life. It was more than just a disturbing sense of *déjà vu*. It was a double vision of myself, like I was living in two planes of existence: the person I was before John, and the person I was forced to become now he had died. The version of me I liked best — the woman who shared her life with the man she loved — was no longer sustainable. She existed in a time beyond my grasp, just as being alive could not help but remind me that John was not. I was alone before John and I was alone again now; once more by myself, yet utterly transformed by those two brief, intense years. Yet I could not ignore the disquieting thought that perhaps no one, not even the people who knew me best, recognised any change in me.

$$\sim\!\!\curlyeqprec$$

Returning to the house after the renderer had completed his work, it was immediately evident that something had changed forever. Inside the shell of my house I felt like an astronaut walking through an alien landscape, denuded of signposts. Was this place safe or threatening? I was scared and excited at once, as if I were walking along a precipice. The only signs of life — that life had taken place in this strange territory — were in the jagged borderlines traced by the point at which the new rendered surface met the rest of the old painted wall. To look at, old and new were clearly distinct areas of each wall; the bottom half of each wall from waist height down to the floor was covered in the matte plaster finish that indicated the extent of Jack's work. But if I closed my eyes and ran my hands over the smooth rendered surfaces, I could not tell where the old painted wall ended and the new rendered surface began.

Only at this moment did I realise how fully I had been using the house as the canvas on which to paint my grief. This was my home, but I could not say any longer that I was quite at home inside it. I could not decide which was more distressing: to see the emptiness of my future life without John presented so literally on these dried and rendered walls; or the awesome privilege of knowing that it was entirely up to me as to what I painted upon them.

Part Four

The Architecture of Pain

17

My perfectly rendered walls soon began to wonder who would paint them. But the prospect of painting the house, the most superficial step in my home's renovation, loomed as yet another round of decision-making. Small decisions about who I should ask to quote on the job. Large decisions about which painter to trust — assuming he was available for the task before the next scheduled appearance of Halley's comet. I was tired of making decisions. Sometimes it seemed I had done little else since the day John died.

Beyond the logistical considerations of paint lay a series of entirely cosmetic choices I would have to make about colour. For once, a sense of abject relief coursed through me when I realised my irresistible renovation force had finally met an immovable object. There was no possible way for me to decide which colours should go on which walls. The risk of error was too high. It was difficult enough selecting a suitable shade of lipstick. Inevitably the colour looked different on my lips from when I first twirled it up out of its tube. My home had too many walls, and they were too big, to be experimenting with erroneous intuition. A large part of my home's beauty is in its architectural details — the original fireplaces and picture rails and ceiling roses — elements that required the assessment of someone who could identify colour schemes to enhance those distinctive features. There was also the outside of the house to consider. I was desperate for a dramatic but elegant colour scheme that showed off the house to its greatest advantage. The house would stand proud and tall in the street, embracing its age at the same time as it put its best architectural foot forward. It would be the Helen Mirren of houses. With these grand ambitions, not even I could fool myself that I had a clue how to proceed, alone, with a few colour charts and a handful of florid swatches to guide me. I would have to abandon myself to the guidance of an expert.

My home's colours were made flesh in the form of Catherine, a consultant recommended by the painter — yet another Irishman — whose price I had eventually agreed to pay. Over the telephone before we met, Catherine advised me to collect a few pages from my favourite interior design and home décor magazines so that during our initial consultation I could demonstrate to her what I liked.

'I need to know whether you prefer your doors treated or untreated, as an example of what I'm talking about,' she said.

Having never given much thought to doors in general, I had no idea what she was talking about, let alone how to answer her question. I suspected it would not be the only time Catherine would leave me speechless. But she was right to assume I had a collection of design, lifestyle and home-improvement magazines close to hand. I had been stockpiling them for some months as grist to my ongoing fantasy of domestic renewal. Here was a task for which I was actually prepared.

At first I tried casually flicking through a few copies of *Vogue Living*, post-it notes at the ready, tagging photographs of painted walls whose colours appealed to me. But casual is something I've never been much good at. I became increasingly excited looking at art-directed scenes that combined the old and the new, the rustic and the contemporary, the chic and the shabby chic. I gorged on images of ottomans, of sumptuous bedroom settings that bore no trace of human occupation, of dinner tables artfully arranged for an intimate dinner party for twelve, of chi-chi sofas strewn effortlessly with cushions from Katmandu and Marrakech. There were not enough pictures for me to gaze at. I vaulted over critical mass completely. I had become addicted to home décor porn.

Without any specific assessment criteria for these images, I was at sea in a flotilla of post-it notes. At the end of this process, I had exhausted several sticky notepads in a variety of colours, and dozens of magazines stared face-up at me from the packing box into which I had carefully placed them. I was sated, but not really satisfied.

'You're not going to show her all this, are you?' asked my friend Sally a few days later, when I lifted the lid of the box to show her what I'd done.

'What do you mean?' I said, pride successfully dinted.

'Don't you think it's a bit . . . excessive?' she said, regarding me with one eyebrow slightly tilted.

Sally is not one to express concern at the drop of a hat. Seeing her eyes flash with alarm, I suddenly realised how this annotated box of home-improvement magazines, tagged and colour-coded, must appear.

'You're right,' I said, laughing quickly to hide my shame. 'I'll have to show her my selected highlights.' I was disappointed. Obsessing about my home was something I thought I had left in my widowhood's wake.

—⟊⟋

Catherine breezed into the house as efficiently and brightly as had the fresh air at its first opportunity to infiltrate the drilled holes in my damp brickwork. She appraised the job in no time, which was just as well at $175 an hour.

'Fabulous house, just wonderful,' she said, her small head darting around quickly in all directions like a peacock on the make. 'The *details* are quite startling, aren't they? Look at this architrave over here. Oh, and this stained internal glasswork. I *love* it! Goodness, *all* these walls were affected? I see what you mean about the size of the job. The damage was extensive, wasn't it? The height, the *height* of these ceilings, Virginia!'

Catherine dragged me through the house like a reluctant pet.

'I say the first thing we need to do is get rid of this eggy colour on the walls,' she said, flicking her wrist at the offending paint. 'It's really . . . well, *eggy*. There's no other word for it. Very early nineties,' she proclaimed, looking over her shoulder at me conspiratorially, as if I understood what she meant.

Still, from my new vantage point at the end of her leash I learned and noticed things about the architecture of my home that I never knew existed. The house had its own dialect, and with Catherine's prompting it began to speak to me: *Architrave, archivolt, cornice, frieze, fluting, gable, pilaster, post and lintel, rosette, travertine.* This new vocabulary of architectural and decorative nouns emerged to supersede the Latinate medical language I had been forced to adopt with John's doctors and nurses, and in which, perversely, I had come to enjoy some minor fluency.

But colour was Catherine's native tongue. She tried teaching me a few words by first speaking in variations of white: *White. White Watsonia. Napkin White. Aran White. Lucent White. Scilly White. Cottontail. Vanilla Frost. Arctic Daisy. Cloudform. Snowy Summit. French Lace. Frosty. Ecru. Dulcimer. Sandshoe. Semi Salted. Sheer Bliss. Millflour. Natura.*

These colours from the palette of 'neutrals' would form our starting point, Catherine told me. I was blinded by so much white. I envied the Inuit, for whom each variation on their words for snow held meaning. The first time I saw the list of colours I misread *Aran White* as *Aryan*. With a triplet of 'k' sounds in my head in the presence of Catherine the Colour Consultant, it was no wonder. But white, it seemed, was no longer just white, even though it was still listed separately. There wasn't even a *Plain*

Vanilla shade. Perhaps *white* was included at the head of the list as a humble launching pad for all the subtle variations marketed with cosmetic-style names, a simple base note for all the *coloratura* that flew high above it. I wondered if someone who was a professional colour connoisseur thought dismissively about plain old white, as if it were the small home town she had long ago left behind.

Later I showed Catherine a selection from my cornucopia of clippings. She looked through the torn pages and immediately noticed things I had not seen for myself. Apparently the clippings expressed my preference for a cool rather than warm colour palette. Catherine's interpretation made me immediately anxious, as if she had identified a(nother) character flaw. I was a cold person; detached, aloof. Or maybe my preference was innate, something I was born with and can't change, like the colour of my eyes. Despite not having given any conscious thought to the wooden doors, I learned that I would prefer them to be painted, rather than to be left in their current untreated state. Catherine's analysis was unnerving. It was too easy for this complete stranger to take a look at a handful of pages torn from magazines and reach conclusions about my aesthetic and personality. I had thought of these pared pages as a random selection. But then I recalled the poet Marianne Moore's line, *Omissions are not accidents*, and felt foolish. Were there other things she could tell about me, I wondered, but decided to keep to herself?

18

When I handed in my paperwork at Los Angeles Airport on our pre-wedding tour in late August 2003, I felt like I had crossed some kind of finish line. The paper trail, the criminal record check, the chest x-ray, the tetanus shot, the final interview at the US Consulate in Sydney — 'Are you, or have you ever been, a member of a terrorist organisation?' — the nearly two thousand dollars in cumulative fees and charges for the privilege, were all complete. The judges' decision was final, and I had passed another test: as far as the US Immigration Service was concerned, I was welcome to become a permanent resident of their country.

Just under one year later, I headed back to New York, but not by choice. The city that had always felt like my second home had now become part of my past, like an old boyfriend. John insisted that I return this time, to apply for a two-year extension to the deadline for taking up the permanent residency my green card bestowed. Due to the strict rules governing these visas, it was imperative that I apply for the extension on US soil.

'I want you to keep your options open,' he said to me as we discussed it again over dinner one night.

'I don't want it,' I said, resisting taking any action to hasten the future that was already arriving too quickly. I baulked at the phrase 'permanent residency', the hubris of the concept.

'You don't know what you'll want to do.'

After I'm dead.

The sentences we spoke in were much longer, but we only uttered aloud the first half of each one. We understood each other perfectly well. I just didn't understand how John could sit there and placidly discuss what I might do with my life after he was dead. But he was adamant that I go.

To leave my husband, even for a short time, made his demise real and inexorable, and my actions somehow complicit in contributing towards a future without him in it. Yet here he was, actively encouraging me to go, *insisting* that I take steps towards securing part of that future.

'Stop worrying. I'll be fine,' he said. 'I've already asked the nurses to see if there's a bed available for me in the palliative care ward.' His mind was made up, even if mine was not.

'But who will look after you if I'm not here?' I said. Even though John's pain was relatively under control at the moment, he needed someone to help him with the tasks of daily life. Without me to look after him, it was not safe for him to be at home.

Finally I suggested flying to the nearest patch of US soil — Honolulu — filling out the paperwork, and flying straight back.

'No, Virginia. I want you to have a break. Go to New York for a few days. Listen to some of that music you love.'

Visions of an unencumbered me traipsing the streets of Manhattan like Marlo Thomas in *That Girl* swam before my eyes and filled me with self-loathing. To fly to America now, to complete this paperwork, felt like giving up on John. There was no corresponding break for him. By sending me away he was committing himself to a week in hospital. Where was the benefit to him in that?

In his next 'Cancer Boy Update' John wrote breezily: 'Virginia leaves for a brief trip to New York in a fortnight's time. I get to go to hospital ("the kennels") as I need 24-hour assistance.' I couldn't help wondering what John's friends, who mostly did not know about my green card, thought of this news. Reading the message, I felt like the quintessential fair-weather wife.

~

A solo trip to New York was a double-edged vacation. Despite my guilt at John being in 'the kennels' I could not deny the sense of relief at having several days to myself. At having a break from the relentless demands of John's disease and concomitant pain. It was not possible to take a break from being John's care-giver without physically being apart from him. And while I often longed for the former, I never wanted the latter. Until this trip my breaks were an occasional Sunday-afternoon walk with a friend while John slept, or getting my legs waxed every four weeks. That felt like enough to me, especially as John never had the opportunity of a break from his pain or from the reality of his disease.

Once there, however, I didn't really know what to do with myself. In the first couple of days, I slept an enormous amount at the SoHo apartment of an old friend and submitted the necessary paperwork for the extension. It felt surreal to be walking around downtown, retracing steps John and I had taken together so recently. I was sick with guilt at being so far away, but my flight had been booked using frequent flier points, and it could not be changed without the sort of expense we could no longer justify now that John wasn't working. I treated myself to a performance of *The Boy from Oz* and was enchanted to watch Hugh Jackman sing and shake his beautiful body in a white skin-tight jumpsuit. He exuded health. A surprisingly moving biographical musical, the show is also in part a love story in which disease takes hold of and destroys the body of one and the lives of both lovers. Watching this unexpected parallel with my own life unfold on stage, I cried nearly as much as I laughed, and ached to go home to John.

~

After one week apart, I couldn't wait to pick up John from hospital and bring him home with me. The separation had been too long. Despite daily phone calls I knew he was keeping from me the true extent of his physical distress. I jumped off the plane, dumped my bags, and drove immediately to the hospital. Rushing into John's room, my heart leapt to see him. *He is alive, he is still here.* We were like puppies in each other's company. It seemed that John had lost some weight, but he still looked at me with those sparkling mischievous eyes, and smiled at me with that boyish grin.

He was my husband and he looked good to me. He held my heart in his delicate hands and I could believe, at least for a while, that everything would be all right.

While I was in New York, John's doctors had decided to take advantage of his enforced stay in hospital to conduct a chest x-ray and an MRI scan to determine whether it would be possible to surgically implant an epidural and drugs pump into his lower spine, in an attempt to arrest the extreme pain he experienced overnight in his legs and lower back due to the growth of the tumours. The primary tumour in his lower back had spread in all directions, and had thickened to the length and width of a loaf of bread. When we had first learned of this surgical pain-relief option months earlier from a pain specialist it had been explained as a method of directly distributing very powerful drugs in low doses, which would save John having to swallow bottles worth of pills each week. At the time it sounded dramatic; now it was our one remaining option. John had been in such acute distress following the MRI scan that neither of us thought much about the chest x-ray, which had been conducted every few months over the course of the year.

Knowing I had just returned from overseas, the resident kindly gave us a few minutes to ourselves before knocking on the door to John's room. Then she walked in and explained the x-ray revealed that the tumours had spread into John's lungs.

We knew this moment would come. We had known to expect cancer to appear in John's lungs ever since the oncologist had laid out these cards for us months earlier. There was a well-established pattern with the type of cancer John had. As the disease became more systemic, first John's mobility would decrease, followed by his ability to fight infection. His appetite would decrease, and finally the tumours would invade his lungs. This was *progress*, as defined by secondary bone cancer and the medical establishment. We just never imagined that this moment would arrive so soon. I felt winded. All I could think of was that I had just spent seven days of whatever time was left available to us on securing my options for life after John was dead. And on sleeping and shopping while John had been in hospital without respite. We just wanted to go home together, have a cup of tea, and talk. We looked at each other and held hands while the resident spoke, much like we did on our wedding day in front of the celebrant. Only it wasn't a beginning the resident spoke of, but the beginning of the end.

19

The sympathy cards flooded my mailbox. There were masses of them, using different combinations of the sub-set of words deemed socially appropriate to the occasion. *Sad. Sorry. Love. Thinking. Brave. Know. Happy. Loss. Heart. Missing. Courage. Friend. Wishing. Always.* Some contained a florid verse composed in a Hallmark office; others bravely expressed themselves in their own hand, whether assured or faltering. Either way, they all said the same thing.

I am so sorry.

The degree of comfort I took from the cards surprised me. It was never the actual words in any particular card that moved me — I was numb to the idea that John's and my friends and family were grieving too — but rather the fact that the sender's thoughts had been put into action. In situations like this it *is* the thought that counts. Cards arrived from people I had never met, but who had known John in England, or Ireland, or through work in Sydney. In our age of lazy electronic communication, I found fleeting moments of morbid pleasure in contemplating the sender's actions, picturing that person selecting, composing and posting her respective card.

As the weeks passed the number of cards became unwieldy to display. Visitors admired the cards *en masse*, but they toppled off the mantelpiece or blew over on the table in the hallway every time I opened the front door. Duplicates soon began to arrive. The fact that the same card was selected by two people who were sometimes very different in sensibility I attributed to the available selection in a given shop or newsagent. Their significance to me was in their cumulative power.

Although proud of the volume of sympathy cards, I found it increasingly difficult to resist the urge to collect and organise them. It was inconceivable that I should just let the cards sit indefinitely on available surfaces. The idea of preserving them in a scrapbook came out of nowhere. I decided to make a book of these cards, to harness their collective emotional force on glossy black quarto-sized pages. Within days I had bought not one, but four large scrapbooks. I had one eye on posterity, and the other on aesthetics: the scrapbooks came in a range of cover designs, but the ones I bought were all of uniform design. A profusion of competing designs would either suggest that I was not serious about my task, or give the false impression that the scrapbooks were about different topics. It was easier to think about how the finished scrapbooks would look on a shelf, than to dwell on the absence to which the cards referred. And while I had already planned the focus for each of the remaining three scrapbooks within the series — one for the photographs of our wedding (we'd never got round to it), our pre-wedding European tour, and a scrapbook I called 'Young John' — there was really only one theme, which the covers needed to reflect.

Thus armed with a publishing strategy for the posthumous scrapbooks, I set to work with the sympathy cards. Immediately

I realised that pasting in the cards one by one would not suffice. There were a number of curatorial decisions to make. At the time these decisions seemed a lot less arbitrary than they turned out to be. For example I first sorted the cards by country of origin. Alphabetically by sender's surname would have been equally justifiable and just as spurious. Cards sent within Australia I sorted according to the age group and category of the sender. Had this person been a colleague of John's? An old family friend of my parents'? Someone who knew us both well? Senders I didn't recognise threw a spanner into my scrapbook works, but I persevered regardless. Only once the categorisation was complete could I begin to assemble the cards within each category. I spread the cards over each double-page layout in the exact order I picked them up from the pile I had made. Two cards with the same design were placed side by side. By the time I had finished pasting all the cards into the pages of the scrapbook it was so pregnant with its contents it had swelled to the size of an open accordion. Who did I think was ever going to look at these cards besides me?

~

As the months passed, my organising principle did not diminish. On the contrary, it became increasingly broad and all-encompassing. If I displayed competence outside in the world of work, I became downright maniacal indoors.

It began innocently enough. First I decided it was time to

make a list of the medicine and medical equipment in the house. Over time we had accumulated an impressive stockpile of prescription medicine along with other flotsam and jetsam relating to John's medication and care: syringes in three different sizes according to which pain-relieving medicine was being injected, alcohol sanitising swabs, bandages of all shapes and sizes for the bedsore on his foot, piles of sterile catheter bags and the Velcro tabs for securing them to his leg. There was also the equipment on loan from Canterbury Hospital that needed returning. The hospital lending pool had other palliative care patients waiting for a shiny spartan hospital bed; or a commode to assist them to take a shower or a shit.

The extent of medical equipment in the house made me think about what else could do with sorting out. I looked around me and saw cupboards and shelves full of John's things that at some point would need going through. There were old address books and packets of photographs, dancing trophies and outdated but expensive camera equipment. There was an old trunk full of LPs he had shipped all the way from London to Sydney but hadn't played in years. And the study was a mess of papers. Because of surgery or chemotherapy he had not filed a tax return for several years, and this year neither of us had given it a thought. We were under siege by his disease, and too busy defending the gates. Wading through years of receipts and bank statements would be another task for me to complete by myself.

I finished the list of the medicine and medical equipment to be returned to the nurses and to the hospital. I made another list for the paperwork and tax returns. There was a list for outside the house, and one for almost every room. Maybe I could replace those dowdy old curtains in the bedroom with shutters. The side gate was a security risk and should be replaced. The more I looked, the more I saw that needed to be opened, identified, arranged, sorted, de-cluttered. The house teemed with the accumulated debris of the years John had lived here. There were cupboards I had never opened, shelves heavy with the weight of unidentified domestic detritus. There were boxes of my own, still unopened, two years after I had moved into the house. There was so much *stuff*. So much to *do*. But none of it was remotely urgent. Only my need to make lists.

—☙

The idea of collecting in one place items from John's childhood and young adulthood began when I found so many of these things while sifting through the domestic rubble of our long-neglected cupboards, shelves and drawers. The archeology of our home revealed many items relating to John's boyhood and young adulthood. There were black-and-white photographs of him as a boy, of his parents, Dennis and Celia, as a young couple, of Fluffy the dog and the council flat he grew up in; there were certificates awarded to John and his sister, Sheila, as teenagers for their ballroom dancing prowess, and others that praised his reading skills or documented his ability to swim fifty yards. Discovering them was like revealing Tutankhamen's tomb: these were precious relics that needed preserving.

Although this process was sometimes therapeutic, gazing at photographs of a young healthy John often rendered me inconsolable and I would stop my project for weeks at a time, leaving handfuls of photographs on top of the cedar sideboard or along the dusty bookshelf where they lay. Sometimes I took care to replace the photographs in their packets, arranging them again neatly in the drawer in which I had found them, even to close the door of the room in which the photographs were kept so I did not have to be reminded of their existence. But whether I saw them or not, in my mind's eye John grinned at me from every photograph. Hope and health yelled from every print. In Kentish Town riding his beloved Ducati motorbike; touring Rome with his best friend, camera slung from his neck; or abseiling from some bridge, decked out in a bright blue helmet and a hideously patterned old sweater. So many photographs, taken a decade, a lifetime, earlier. He had travelled to all corners of Europe, with friends and with his former wife. How I envied the physical freedom these photographs revealed, and the time desultorily spent in ignorance of a future in which time would simply run out. The sun shone brightly outside but I remained indoors, sifting through a life with John that I never knew, mourning the loss of the things we had, and the future life that could never be ours. The 'Young John' scrapbook became a place I created as somewhere for him to exist. In the pages of this scrapbook he was healthy, fit, happy, vital. He was alive.

The one thing I could not do was throw out his clothes. There were old t-shirts and boxer shorts, a linen bag full of socks, and a collection of outlandish ties I'd never really liked. There were casual trousers he hadn't worn in months because the tumour in his right thigh had swelled the top of his leg so much that he could no longer wear anything but a pair of tracksuit pants that originally belonged to me; I had unwittingly stretched their elasticised waist for him through years of wear, making them his most comfortable trousers because they did not pinch into his primary tumour. There were shirts we had bought together, shirts I had bought him while we were in Europe, and old shirts that had spent a lot more time with him than I had.

I had read so often in books of a grieving person who buries their face in their loved one's clothes and greedily drinks in their scent. But I was shocked to discover that John's clothes carried only the faintest whiff of him. Maybe I don't have much of a sense of smell, but no matter how deeply I inhaled I just couldn't smell him. I was like an airport sniffer dog trained to identify a scent whose trail had gone cold. The more I sniffed the more palpable his absence became. I was bereft: I had planned to smell him on those clothes forever.

I wondered if John's smell lingered in the business shirts and suits we had given to charity. His corporate clothes were the one part of John's wardrobe that was no longer at home. One day a few months after he stopped working at the office he surprised me by announcing that he would like to donate them all to St Vincent de Paul.

'Are you sure?' I asked him, not sure I could countenance such selfless practicality.

'Well, I'm not going to wear them anymore, am I?' was all he said. 'Maybe it will help some poor bugger get a job.'

I pulled out the flock of white business shirts to show him, possibly in an effort to demonstrate that he didn't need to give all of them away. There were at least a dozen of them. But John was adamant: all but one shirt went into the box that the charity would collect from our doorstep as soon as I called to arrange it.

Out went his business suits as well, all except for one. We kept the suit he married me in. Given that by then John was spending the vast bulk of his time in a pair of tracksuit pants, even I had to admit that, given a choice, it was unlikely that John would wear a suit.

In fact, his wedding suit was the last thing he wore.

20

A height-adjustable hospital bed. At first I didn't understand what the nurses meant. For a moment I pictured our queen-sized mattress atop some contraption that the palliative care nurses raised and lowered at their will and command. Then I understood what they really wanted: to replace the bed John and I shared as husband and wife with a slimline chrome bed with levers and angles and removable rails. They wanted to transform our bedroom into a domestic version of a hospital room, with this clinical bed front and centre.

The nurses insisted that the bed's manoeuvrability would minimise the potential pain for John's care-givers as they — we — transferred him in and out of the wheelchair. They mentioned there was such a bed available for long-term loan in the hospital's lending pool. They had done their homework. The nurses, like the doctors in the palliative care ward we had recently come home from, were behaving as if John had only months to live.

'It will be much better,' one nurse said to us as we stared, wide-eyed at the hospital bed hovering like a ghost in front of us.

Better for whom? I wanted to ask. Not for John. Not for me. Not for a newlywed couple. This was one more change we could never have anticipated. One more change we absolutely did not want. Our queen-sized bed, despite its artificially undulating, bedsore-preventing mattress and consequent mismatched head heights, was *ours*. We lay down together in it each night, and we woke in it each morning. We had enjoyed plenty of fun in this bed, and shed tears in it too. Neither John nor I wanted the hospital bed in our bedroom. But one moment of unnecessary pain was equally intolerable.

Within minutes I realised there was room for only one person in the hospital bed. Where would *I* sleep? There would not be enough room for both our queen-sized bed and the hospital bed in our bedroom. The nurses wanted to cast me out on my own. It was too soon. John and I had only been married for seven months. I wanted to spend the rest of my life with him. But this threat of forced physical separation felt like a death. Not even an old couple, a couple who have been married for decades, should have to face these changes. Certainly not a man of forty-seven and his thirty-four-year-old wife.

As normal as possible, for as long as possible.

'No bloody way,' said John at the first inkling of the nurses' plan.

'I don't think so,' I said when I realised the implications for our sleeping arrangements.

We resisted the idea of the adjustable hospital bed for as long as we could. But to the nurses, ultimately our 'no' didn't really mean 'no'. They knew they would win, and proceeded to organise delivery of the hospital bed.

'We're simply not allowed to lift John in and out of bed like you do,' they said to me, drawing the ace of insurance from their metaphorical coat sleeves.

~

If we were going to continue sleeping in the same room, there was only one thing to do: buy a single bed for me.

I responded to this massive new disruption to our lives in my usual fashion, by acting immediately. The next available lunch hour I headed to the bedroom furniture department at David Jones to buy a single bed. Outside, Sydney's central business district might have been swilling with cars and buses and pedestrians, but the display floor was as quiet as the grave. Arranged over a broad expanse were chests of drawers, bedroom settings, stand-alone mirrors, divans and mattresses, all monitored by two bored-looking sales people. They would glance up occasionally from whatever it was they were doing at the central desk, like a couple of horses grazing in one corner of a huge paddock. Looking for the bittersweet spot in the cavernous room that housed single beds, I naively assumed there would be one or two styles from which to choose. What I discovered was a bewildering selection of single beds in a variety of styles with prices to match.

It had been much longer than I remembered since I had bought a bed. For many years, I had slept soundly on the understanding that a king was a king, a queen a queen, and so on. What in the world was a *king single*? At some point in the previous decade, royalty had entered the humble quarters of the single bed. I looked around for a queen single as a point of comparison, without success. The bedding range on display at David Jones offered no gradations of royalty, or even minor aristocracy — no mattress bore the appellation 'prince', 'earl', or 'duchess'. There was just the king single bed, or the plain old single bed. Somehow the bedding industry had approved this vocabulary to persuade the likes of me to consider switching to the larger size. The king single is visibly larger. In terms of length and width, it's good to be the king. I was thrown by the number of choices I was going to need to make.

I plonked down on one of the king single beds and tried to imagine how it would look in our bedroom, squashed up against the hospital bed. Already I could tell the beds would be of different heights. Maybe the adjustability of John's hospital bed wouldn't be such a bad thing after all. As I perched on the edge of a single mattress, lost in a haze of fluorescent lighting and fear, a well-heeled professional couple approached me. Could they tell I was being forced to buy one of these beds to sleep on alone? I felt sick at the thought they might try to make eye contact. But they only had eyes for the king single bed to my left. *For our five-year-old*, they explained to the sales assistant, who had trotted over to meet them. Knowing smiles all round.

They were buying a bed for their child. My husband had just received his own single bed, on loan. He will slowly die in that bed,

I thought, and I will watch him from my new single bed. This was not what I planned when I married John, even though I knew he had cancer. This was not how I imagined our married life would unravel. Here, at the foot of a single bed, the lights in the display area shining more harshly than ever, the reality of John's sudden decline felt like a slap in the face. *I chose this bed*, I thought, blinking back tears of self-pity, *and now I'm about to lie in it*.

I had to get away from the couple. Their arrival in my corner of the display floor felt like a violation of my privacy. Like Goldilocks, I moved from one bed to another, bouncing gently up and down on the edge of each mattress to test my degree of comfort. I was going through the motions: I knew that none of them would feel just right.

Eventually I wandered over to the sales assistant, who seemed a little apprehensive. I must have looked as miserable as I felt. She perked up when I told her I wanted to buy a bed. To indicate the bed I had selected, I deliberately used my left hand, counter to my right-hander's natural preference. It was important to me that she saw the wedding band on the ring finger of my left hand. I realised I wanted her to assume I was inquiring about the bed on behalf of a child connected to me in some undefined way. A child John and I would never have. Undefined, unborn.

While finalising the transaction I imagined an alternate life with John in which time would unfold like a story well told, one year after another, each one bringing with it new joys and challenges.

It was a fleeting luxury to consider the future as a place to plan for, as a knot at the end of all the multiple strands of the shared life towards which we worked and paid off debts and bent our dreams. Increasingly the future appeared to me like the Russian steppe, a flat, vast, undifferentiated expanse. Cold world without end.

~

Within days our bedroom's inevitable transformation was complete. Although the reaches of our private world were contracting, our bedroom — like the universe — seemed to be expanding. Otherwise how could it accommodate all the furniture and medical equipment now required to be part of the life of this most intimate yet public space?

Our mattress now rested against a wall of the spare room, a dethroned queen. When I dismantled our former marital bed, John and I had been shocked to see the effects of rising damp clearly evident in our bedroom. Unbeknown to us, the paint had long been bubbling and peeling directly behind our bed, low to the ground and out of sight. The water damage along that wall was much worse than we had imagined. Piles of plaster dust and paint peelings lay on the carpet where they had fallen, out of reach of the vacuum. I cleaned up the evidence, but we both knew the plaster would continue to crumble, and the walls to slowly weep.

I was right to suspect we could not sleep side by side. At first we had moved one of the bedside tables and pushed my bed up against John's hospital bed, but immediately it became clear that we would not be able to enjoy even that degree of compromised proximity: a corridor wide enough for the wheelchair to manoeuvre John in and out of bed demanded our two beds be separated. No matter how hard we tried to stay together, some new physical law forced us apart, as if we were two positively charged atoms.

In bed that night, from my position hard up against the wall beneath the windows on one side of the room, I looked across at my husband over the paraphernalia on the remaining bedside table between us, over the books and medicines and CDs and sweets and the notepad on which he charted his pain.

'It's all right, gorgeous girl,' John said. 'As long as we're together — that's the main thing, isn't it?' He smiled his accepting smile, hard-won from years of fighting, and I felt bad for my petty envies. We were alive, we were together, the bedroom was still ours to share. But John's hospital bed was now centre stage, and I occupied a front-row seat for his final act.

21

One night several months after John died I stayed up later than usual. For once I was physically tired when I padded into the bedroom and flicked on the light switch.

Instantly I was aware I was not alone. There, a metre above the bed that John and I used to share — the queen ensemble my father and I had restored to its original position in the first week of my widowhood — was one of the largest and most beautiful butterflies I had ever seen. It seemed to have arrived out of nowhere.

As large as an outstretched hand, the butterfly had settled into position on the wall just above our bedhead, exactly in the middle. It was still, but very much alive, its wings pulsing with a slight but discernible movement like waves of heat. I was stunned by its colour, a base of thick, luxuriant black, flecked with a brilliant orange that looked splashed on, like a Jackson Pollock canvas. What struck me most was the feeling that the butterfly had been waiting for me.

Without skipping a beat, I started talking to it as I began to undress for bed.

'Well, how are you?' The words came naturally, just as if John himself were in our bedroom and we were alone again together. 'I didn't notice you come in. Were you out in the garden?' I chatted as if it were nothing unusual to be talking to an enormous butterfly perched above my bed.

'There's no pain, is there? I know I have to think that, but I feel it, too.' It was so exciting to think of how freely the butterfly could move, effortlessly flying wherever it wanted.

Sleepiness overwhelmed me almost immediately, as if a spell had been cast.

'I hope you know how happy I am to see you,' I said. 'You promised you would watch over me, if you could. I will always love you and I miss you so much.'

I looked intensely at the beautiful butterfly one more time, trying to imprint the vision on my memory forever before switching off the light. During the minute or so that had passed, the butterfly had not budged from the position it had been in when I first noticed it.

The instant the room was dark, the butterfly took flight. I heard its gentle whirring but couldn't believe my ears when I realised it had actually landed on the pillow next to the one my head lay on. In the days when John and I shared this bed that pillow would have been mine, but over the past few months I had migrated to what used to be John's side of the bed. I'd never been this close to such a large butterfly before. Instinctively I flinched; my arm accidentally nudged the pillow and after a pause the butterfly took flight. I felt bad to have cut short the coda to this extraordinary experience. Before falling asleep I wondered if the butterfly had been trying to kiss me goodnight.

The next thing I knew it was three or four o'clock in the morning and I needed to go to the toilet. In the dim moonlight coming through the living room windows I spotted something lying on the polished wooden floorboards. It was far too small to be the butterfly; its shape was more like one of the dried leaves that curl up and blow into the house underneath the front door as the wind screams down our street. I wondered briefly where the butterfly had gone before returning to bed.

The next morning I emerged from the bedroom and stopped in my tracks. What I'd thought was a dried leaf on my floorboards was actually a fat, dull-grey bogong moth, curled lifeless on the ground. No colour, no movement. It was just a broken carcass, a physical framework that no longer functioned. Whatever life had been within that shell had been outgrown and discarded. Looking at that dead moth, I quickened with the certainty that wherever John is now, he is as free and vital and colourful as the exotic butterfly.

How the butterfly entered and left my home remains a mystery. I have not seen it since that night, nor do I expect ever to see it again. But it helps me to know that he's flying.

22

The pain chart on John's bedside table was our Book of Days. The handwritten notes chronicled the life and times of pain, the unpredictable and jealous chaperone of our marriage.

Pain told John when he would sleep and when he would wake. It dictated when he felt like talking, or eating, or getting out of the house. It determined when I could have a conversation with him that did not revolve around medication. John was regularly in so much physical distress that he needed what are known as 'breakthrough' doses of morphine, over and above his usual prescribed medications. The reason for each breakthrough, the time of day it was administered, and in what dosage, were what the doctors wanted us to record. This bedroom bureaucracy was a more difficult task than you might imagine. When your husband is in agony at three in the afternoon or four o'clock in the morning, and you're responsible for injecting a dose of narcotics that will hopefully alleviate the pain, neither of you is focused on documenting the experience.

As the primary tumour expanded in his lower back and the secondary tumours invaded his thigh bones, disease distorted John's posture. As the loaf-shaped primary tumour continued to morph and twist John's spine, so his right thigh kept expanding from the effects of metastatic growth. The perverse width of his upper leg was confusing to the eye, which intuitively compared it with the increasingly thin body of which it was part. This was clearly unnatural growth. For months now John had slept propped up at a forty-five-degree angle on a complex arrangement of pillows and cushions. Just one cushion even slightly out of place could induce unbearable pressure on the protruding tumour. Like an origami expert I could organise his cushions the way he needed them within seconds; the professional carers didn't stand a chance of meeting our exacting standards. But without the cushions where he needed them, John simply could not get comfortable enough to drift off. The primary tumour in John's lumbar spine had grown so big that it began pushing against the commode's plastic straps. In desperation one day I hacked off one of the straps with a kitchen knife. To hell with the hospital equipment lending pool, I thought. They don't have to endure this pain, or watch the person they love endure it.

So we monitored John's daily battle with pain as closely as others watched their stock portfolios rise and fall. Our pain calendar helped the doctors understand that John felt pain in his thigh mostly during the afternoon; and pain in his right foot in the evening when he was in the wheelchair but not while in bed; and pain in the lower back that caused him to wake during the night. Recorded over periods of weeks, patterns unrecognisable at our close proximity became apparent to his specialists, who used the knowledge gained from our pain chart to titrate his mix of medicines. Focused on the local issues, we failed to notice the global one.

~

Dixon described himself as an 'old school' kind of doctor. Given that John and I had waited for five weeks to see him in his crowded rooms, ensconced like a squirrel in his burrow, we had expected at least an introduction. Not only did the surgeon not identify himself to us — really, he could have been anyone, this gruff aging man in a white coat surrounded by medical journals and token photographs of family members (Were they his, I wondered, or generic smiling faces provided at some medical specialists' supply store?) — but his face betrayed no change in expression during our first perfunctory interview with him. He seemed to consider uttering a simple 'hello' or 'goodbye' not a matter of common courtesy, but a sign of weakness.

The purpose of our meeting was for Dixon to outline the steps involved in surgically implanting a titanium reservoir, about the size of a small silver bell you ping for attention at an unattended reception, into John's abdomen with a spinal catheter. The pump distributed extremely potent pain-relieving medication directly into his spinal fluid via a catheter connected to the pump's reservoir. As we had learned months earlier in our first exposure to the world of pain management, this surgical procedure was the pain relief of last resort.

My impression was that the surgeon was used to dealing with a lot of workers compensation cases involving people with bad backs and poor English. John made the cardinal error of being articulate about his own pain. He was able to describe physical sensations using adjectives rather than hand gestures. He asked questions about the surgery. How often had this doctor performed this invasive procedure? What possible side-effects could John expect? What was his success rate with this surgery, and what were the risks of infection? What medication would be contained in the reservoir, and how would it be replenished?

These questions did not seem improper or impudent. On the contrary, they were basic and crucial to our understanding of what was likely to be the next major hurdle in John's palliative care. But Dixon seemed miffed that we asked anything of him at all. Perhaps we should have just been thankful that he deigned to have us in his rooms. Nobody had suggested we genuflect on arrival.

We left that appointment with the impression that the surgeon did not quite believe John was in the level of acute pain to which he, and I, and all his other pain specialists and nurses, attested. If John had flailed his arms around, moaned a lot, and feigned a lack of understanding during this first meeting, perhaps Dixon would have taken as seriously as we did John's level of physical distress. I have no doubt that this surgeon would be calling for a scalpel himself had he to endure what John did every day. With or without documentation.

~

Around this time I started flicking through the writings of Wittgenstein in an effort to help me think about physical pain. Reality had become impossible to process: I needed the comfort of abstraction, my intellectual high ground. The gulf between the experience of pain, and its perception and interpretation through language, by self and by others, was at the core of Wittgenstein's philosophical investigations. John never batted an eyelid when I spread out my Wittgenstein books on the coffee table, sat down on the floor beside him in his wheelchair, and began scribbling in my notebook. He understood how my brain worked, that I needed something — anything — to help make sense of what was happening to him, and to us. John had pills to swallow and narcotics coursing through his bloodstream for his pain. I had philosophy for mine. But there was little consolation.

The days grew shorter as we approached winter, and we liked huddling together in the living room. While it was no longer possible to cuddle on the sofa, we sat as close as the wheelchair allowed. Next to my philosophy textbooks propped on the coffee table were John's feet, encased in protective swatches of sheepskin that were secured over each foot with a thick Velcro tab. His booties, as we called them, were a recent addition to his wardrobe. As unattractive as they sound, the booties were an object of envy at the pain specialist's clinic, where other patients regularly asked John where he had found them. Function won out over style when it came to the booties, which were designed to alleviate a painful sensation in John's feet. He likened it to the feeling of pushing down hard on a stirrup beneath each foot, instead of the flat footrests of his wheelchair against which his feet actually rested. He had no feeling in his feet anymore; this pain was neurological. But the sheepskin seemed to help.

From time to time John would ask me to rearrange his legs on the table, as they did not like being in the one place for an extended period. One evening as I got up from my position cross-legged on the floor beside him, I noticed behind John's wheelchair a particularly high pile of plaster dust on one side of the fireplace. Following its trail, I saw that an entire chunk of the lower section of one wall had disappeared into dust. This rising damp was gaining serious momentum. John, looking in the opposite direction towards the television, couldn't see behind him and decided my claims were probably exaggerated. But once I had noticed the damage, I became convinced that over the last few weeks the rising damp had worsened. Then again, every time John pointed out a new bump on his body I silently pictured it as a mass of cancerous tissue waiting to be revealed on his next x-ray. It was probably just as well he thought I was being overly dramatic.

Wittgenstein argued that the vagueness of our concept of pain reflects the uncertainty of language in general. To Wittgenstein, nothing is outside or beyond language. On a rational level I could accept and understand that, nodding sagely as I pored over his influential texts and wrote down phrases as if they were life-buoys. But reading him as the wife of someone enduring daily and nightly agony, it seemed to me that some forms of pain are beyond conceptualisation, much further beyond expression. Wittgenstein maintained that to speak of pain is one of the most difficult linguistic activities. The act of expressing pain depends on the speaker's skill as well as the types of expressions available for expressing pain. Expressions that are understood by the person to whom one is speaking. Whether that person is a spouse or a medical specialist. John and I reached a point of understanding in which a slight grimace, or a period of silence, would be enough for me instinctively to reach a conclusion about what and where John's pain was at any given time. But on many occasions, I was at a loss to know what sort of discomfort he was in, and he was in too much pain to articulate it. John's face would betray no discomfort and yet his legs felt full of shooting arrows. If pain is beyond expression, is it necessarily beyond the capacity of an intimate observer to understand it? I thought of how many other experiences in life that are beyond expression — hearing a passage of music and being profoundly moved; or looking at my husband and knowing that the words 'I love you' are totally inadequate to convey exactly what I mean. But in attempting to write about grief, and about love, I suspect some experiences are beyond language. I think Wittgenstein assumes too much, asks too much, of words.

—❧

On the day of John's surgery we were full of hope and apprehension. The glimmering promise of tangible pain relief was balanced by the usual anxieties of preparing John for hospital, and preparing us both for the bureaucracy of hospital admission.

After trawling through the administrative nets of admission to hospital and answering the same questions from multiple different nurses, John was moved onto the hospital bed from his wheelchair by way of an enormous mechanical hoist complete with levers and even stirrups for the patient's legs. It looked like a swing set for grown-ups. John and I exchanged glances and tried not to laugh: at home I lifted him in and out of bed every day in a matter of less than a minute. Watching three nurses struggle to determine the most efficacious method for preserving their backs and minimising John's pain as they transferred him seemed like a live-action variation on one of those light-bulb-changing jokes. The complicated manoeuvre took the nurses almost half an hour. Once in the hospital bed, John was changed into a blue surgical gown and wheeled down into the pre-operating area. I kissed him and waved as he was pushed around a corner, out of sight, for his anesthetic.

While the operation to insert the pump would take only half an hour, John would be in recovery for several hours. And without anything specific to do for him, I found myself for once at something of a loss. Deciding I just couldn't wait long hours in an empty hospital room despite the books and everything I had brought to distract me, I drove home to do some laundry. *Rinse and repeat.* A load of washing seemed easier than sitting doing nothing, or trying to feign interest in watching the Olympic Games that were being relentlessly broadcast on the tiny hospital-room screen.

~

The water was rising in the washing machine when the phone rang. It was the nursing sister.

'Virginia, are you far away?' she said.

'Why? What's happened?' Immediately I panicked at the thought that something had gone wrong, but couldn't imagine what could have changed in twenty-five minutes. The surgery wasn't even due to start for another half an hour.

'Can you come and collect John?'

'Is the operation — is there a problem? I thought —'

'No. Well, yes. Well, Doctor Dixon has cancelled the operation.'

'What?' I couldn't quite process what she was telling me. The news obeyed no logic.

Dixon never mentioned once prior to the operation that we should make sure John's nurses avoided his abdomen as a site for inserting the needles that attached to his syringe-driver. Looking at a couple of red and irritated patches on John's pale belly, the surgeon felt they presented too great a risk of infection during or after surgery to go ahead with the procedure.

The cancellation of John's operation was more than I could bear. I didn't know whether to scream or cry. The hours involved in preparing and admitting John to hospital, all for nothing. No relief from John's pain, or from constant disappointment. No relief from the fact that he was dying. *Rinse and repeat.* It wasn't so much the setback of why the procedure had been cancelled, or when or even if we could try again; it was the final straw of having to undo and redo all the minutiae surrounding John's hospital visit that completely floored me. Packing up all his medicines, the careful composition of the items he needs to be relatively comfortable in his wheelchair; the sheer effort of moving him into and out of the car; carrying and wheeling a suitcase, my handbag, and pushing John in his chair — none of these things I thought of specifically at the time, but their cumulative weight was at that point just too heavy.

John was much more sanguine about the latest setback than I was, but we were both very deflated when we got home. Knowing that many of our friends and family would want to find out how the surgery went, I sent a text message announcing the operation had been cancelled and that I'd be in touch soon. Anger was not an emotion that came easily to me. But at that moment there was no doubt I was too angry to speak to anyone.

~

The next morning, I opened my eyes and wished I hadn't. It was the very first time I had looked at John and wished I wasn't there, wished I did not have to move from my bed and spend most of my time tending to his every need. Wished that he were healthy, that we could just live like any other newlywed couple. It scared me to feel that I could not face the day ahead, that for the first time I had nothing left.

'The more I do or try to do for you, the less it seems to make any difference. We're going backwards!' I wept with frustration where I lay, too enervated to raise my head from the pillow of my single bed.

John, sitting up in his hospital bed across from me, could cope with anything except seeing me upset.

'Are you . . . angry with me, Virginia?' he said, his eyes wet with confusion and, ever so faintly, the fear of abandonment that haunted him.

'I am not angry with you,' I said, my heart breaking to see that look on his face. 'None of this is your fault. We are in this together, darling. We're a team. You and me. I'm not going anywhere. I made that promise to you. It is just so frustrating not to be able to do anything!'

It was impossible for me to be angry with John. He did not ask for this disease, for enduring pain. My anger was directed at circumstance, at fate, at cancer, and at the medical practitioners who kept robbing us of hope. I got out of my bed and moved those few steps — so near, so far away — to his. We hugged each other and cried, understanding that we were each doing our best.

~

Two weeks later John finally had the operation. In his next 'Cancer Boy Update', he announced to his friends that he was pleased to be able to call himself a 'bionic man':

> The operation went well and the pain is finally getting under control. I now have two pumps to carry around — one inside me and the other in my little navy handbag. The external one is being used as a regulator, so that the morphine can have its doses changed easily by the nursing staff, after consultation with either me, or a doctor. I am going to be sad giving me navy handbag back.

~⁓

After John became the Bionic Man and his pain, while still debilitating, was under much better control than it had been for months, we were eager to get out of the house. I had looked forward to taking daytrips in the car with John to places in and around Sydney, but when I raised this with him John confessed that he preferred to stay close to home.

One of our favourite destinations was the Opera House. For a pair of music lovers, it was one performance space that was not only reliably accessible for a wheelchair user, but also a venue that hosted concerts we actually wanted to attend. Our last trip there was to see the Australian Chamber Orchestra perform the music of Astor Piazzolla, featuring accordionist James Crabbe. As usual, I rang the venue in advance to organise our seating arrangements. While the staff there were always helpful, the fact remained that we couldn't sit close enough together to hold hands. I sat on an aisle seat and John sat in his wheelchair across from me next to the wall. So as not to be an inconvenience to other patrons. No matter how accommodating the Opera House was, our experience confirmed that the world is constructed by able-bodied people for able-bodied people.

I never saw John as 'sick' so it always surprised me how often I caught people staring at us when we were out together. John never seemed to notice them. I suppose by the time of that concert he looked very frail indeed. We ran into acquaintances during the interval. 'Oh, you've taken on a lot,' the woman said, looking at me with a mixture of admiration and horror, while we waited in line to buy drinks. I had heard a few variations on this theme by now: 'I don't know if I could do what you do' or 'You're very brave' or 'I don't know how you do it'. Often these comments came from the nurses who saw people caring for someone they loved every day. Even my mother, who selflessly cooked and cleaned and washed and ironed and tended and mended for my brother and me for years, often shook her head gently and said, 'I don't know how you manage.'

I appreciated these comments but to me they sounded as if being with John were a job I'd applied for. I was so proud to be married to John. I loved looking over at him during a concert and watching the pure enjoyment on his face as he took everything in. *This is my husband.* I admired him so much for being fully present, wherever we were. I envied his ability to focus and to forget everything else. I spent so much time in my head.

~

Now John was sleeping better at night, I was not. I started waking at three, four o'clock in the morning, impossibly alert, thinking about his funeral. But he was still alive, breathing in the bed just across from mine. Tossing and turning, my mind racing, eventually I got up and tried watching television, making a cup of tea, writing clichés about love and loss in the journal I sporadically kept. I even attempted editing the manuscript that a writer friend had sent me in the hope that I'd welcome the distraction; seeing what fit and what didn't. But the words swam in front of my eyes.

Returning sleeplessly to bed, I watched John as he slept and tried to imagine myself addressing the people who have come to say goodbye to him. Will I be too overwhelmed with grief to speak, or so stunned that I will reveal barely any emotion at all? What could I possibly say to these people? I am terrified I won't do justice to him. I kept thinking of things to include, and pictured myself trying to keep it together as I face this crowd, full of John's life, without him directly by my side. What will I wear? A new dress, or something I have worn before — to work, a party, a christening?

It appalled me that John was lying a few feet away and I was thinking about what to wear to his funeral. *He's not dead yet, you heartless bitch.* The facts of John's impending death were staring me in the face, yet it was beyond my wildest late-night imaginings to picture the reality of his absence. How could I possibly sum up his life? How does anyone sum up their own life, let alone that of the person they love most in the world?

23

After six months there were still no words chiselled into the headstone that marked John's grave. Trying to find the words for something for which there were none had proven too difficult. As a former book editor, my skill had always been in revising other people's words, not coming up with my own. For me, John's gravestone was proving to be the ultimate blank slate.

In the days after John's death the Necropolis at Rookwood Cemetery had sent me a bundle of paperwork including a certificate with my name on it. I wondered if it was an encouragement award for breathing, for staying upright. Before I saw its title I could tell by its thick embossed paper and creamy colour that this was no ordinary piece of correspondence.

The document was a formal certification of my 'right of burial' with John in Plot 943. I couldn't help but chuckle. I didn't know which was more amusing — the knowledge that I had my very own plot of ground to be buried in, or that the document specified that, when the time came, I would be lowered into the ground on top of my husband. There mustn't be enough room anymore for side-by-side burials. Land is too valuable to be wasted on the dead, especially in a booming real-estate market. All I could hear was John's voice saying, 'Well if you're going to be lying on top of me, make sure you're facing down.'

I now had a title deed I never expected. Alive or dead, I would never be homeless. It would be important to hold on to this document. I would have to keep it in a safe place until the time someone else needed to present it on my behalf. But I had a feeling that I would be a picture of rude health for long years to come.

Since the funeral I had carried with me a small notebook in which I tried variations on my morbid theme. I scribbled all the permutations of phrases I could think of, until I had a requiem's worth of words. I drew the outline of the headstone and tried arranging words inside it, to better judge what they might look like once chiselled into place. My notebook is full of cemetery scribble and sketches of headstones.

Here are some of the phrases I jotted in my notebook:

A wonderful man
Beloved husband
Beloved husband of Virginia
Adored beloved husband
Loving brother
Loving friend
Loved and respected
Loved by all
Loved by all who knew him
Deeply loved, respected and missed
Trusted friend

I miss you every day

Always missed

You will be missed always

Greatly missed

Sadly missed

Missed by all who knew him

Admired and sadly missed always

Admired and sadly missed by all who knew him

Never forgotten

A life of love and laughter cut sadly short

One theme and a hundred empty variations. There were times I wished that John had chosen cremation.

The editorial queries ran through my mind. I wondered whether it was overly self-referential to name myself on the stone. If I needed to name John's parents — both long deceased — individually, or at all. If it was important to name London and Sydney as the cities where John was born and where he died; or just the years.

I also had the word limit to contend with. Another document in my correspondence from Rookwood Cemetery stated that eighty letters were included in the price of the burial plot. (I couldn't help but think of all those advertisements on daytime television: '*But wait! You also get a free set of steak knives …*') To exceed eighty letters would cost me sixty cents per letter. But was 'the' or 'a' counted in the first eighty letters? Did the space between words count as one letter? Was a hyphen treated as a letter? What about numerals, for the years of birth and death? I imagined some shadowy figure at the Necropolis solemnly counting the letters on draft texts submitted by the Bereaved.

Wandering around John's new neighbours one day for inspiration, I was astonished to discover that even in a cemetery the words have a house style. They all begin in the same vein — loving wife, devoted father, beloved brother, sister, son-in-law. Like Noah's Ark, the words went on to the stones two by two. The adjectives felt forced, as if the writer was trying to convince the reader that their subject was worthy of a stranger's pause. Each person sounded the same as the next. But John was not the same as his neighbours. His stone had to say something different.

My metaphorical blue pencil was never far away. I spied the description 'Special Angel' on one headstone. That's quite a claim, I thought, but does Angel really need to be capitalised? Another announced that Jose was now 'Among the angels . . . at peace, at rest. In Gods' care'. I flinched: the apostrophe was in the wrong spot. Poor Jose. His Catholic family had announced that he was now in the care of multiple gods, rather than the one god he was purported to believe in. What Jose needed was the loving care of a proofreader. Renewing my faith in apostrophes gave me strength.

Until then I hadn't considered the possibility of a spelling mistake, or a grammatical error. Suddenly I realised how easy it was to do: one missing letter and I could bequeath John a *trusted fiend* or a *loving bother*. I wondered if I should offer my services to the Necropolis.

Spotting others' errors was much easier than coming up with words of my own. In editing books or writing reports, words were revised, rearranged, deleted. But for this editorial job, the stonemason's chisel was mightier than my pencil. I would see the same words, in the same order, every time I visited John's grave.

'Just write *something*,' I heard him say in my head. 'It's not *me*. It's not *us*. I don't care what you put on it, just get the details down and be done with it.'

John was right. No one else would pay the inscription as much attention as I. What I had been agonising over, ostensibly on John's behalf, was for my own benefit. How was it possible to summarise the life of the handsome forty-seven-year-old I had married? My attempt would stare back at me for the term of *my* natural life. I should have written it *this* way instead. It would be better if I had left *that* out. What sort of wife was I if I couldn't come up with words for John's headstone? I never thought I would be a wife. Yet here I was, suddenly a widow. An editor without a text.

~

Eventually I sent some words off to the Necropolis on the form they had enclosed months earlier with my Right of Burial certificate.

They would never be perfect, I decided, but they would have to do. I asked for, and received, a proof before the stonemason went to work with his chisel, so I could check it one last time.

By the time I signed the proof and faxed confirmation back to the Necropolis, John had been dead and buried eight months, and I had trudged through a lot of paperwork regarding his estate. Banks, insurance companies, financial institutions — they all required copies of his birth certificate and death certificate. The years tolled like bells in my head.

I didn't notice the error until I had visited John's grave, complete with inscribed stone, a couple more times. Something about the year 1957 didn't seem right. I looked at the inscription again. A knot of anguish formed in my stomach and slowly tightened. At the same time I hoped desperately to be wrong, I saw that I had given John the incorrect birth year. I had confused the fact that he was forty-seven when he died, with the 1956 that was his actual birth year. Or it could have been because I knew he had fought cancer for seven years. I had insisted on a proof from the cemetery to avoid the stonemason making a mistake. It never occurred to me that I might make one myself. Everyone agreed that John had died too young. In my unconscious editorial wisdom I had made him one year younger, bestowing an extra year of life we could never share. My blue pencil could change anything, it seemed, except the truth.

24

'Hey, sexpot, you awake?' I nudged open the bedroom door with the breakfast tray that held our tea, my toast, and John's cereal. We measured our life not in coffee spoons, but in bowls of Coco-Pops. 'John? Wake up! Breakfast.'

John stirred and opened one eye dubiously. He winced from the pain that arrived with consciousness, then smiled obligingly.

'Wifey,' he said, letting out a sigh as he spotted the tray. 'How the devil are you?' He couldn't have been less interested in breakfast.

Despite our trips to the supermarket and efforts to find restaurants that were accessible, John was rapidly losing interest in food.

I looked at him perched against his pillows. Suddenly he looked so very thin. I hadn't really noticed it before. Even though he had lost weight over the course of the year, for some reason this morning he looked dramatically thinner. It was as if the weight had been stolen from his shoulders overnight, like an expensive coat, when we weren't looking.

While John's weight loss was only just dawning on me, I had slowly grown aware of his decreasing appetite. He never seemed to feel hungry anymore or to even think about food at all. The first change I observed was a decline in how much wine he drank.

Whereas previously we didn't think twice about downing a bottle between us at dinnertime, I began to notice that when I reached for a refill, John's glass wasn't much emptier than when I'd first filled it. Next came the realisation that food itself wasn't of much interest to him anymore. At breakfast he dutifully polished off some tea and a slice of toast, or a sugar-laden bowl of Coco-Pops, but he could not offer any suggestions as to what he would like for lunch. He wasn't remotely fussy about what I left for him in the brown bar-fridge when I wasn't there, or when his work colleagues weren't dropping by with sushi or a sandwich. By dinnertime the thought of food was completely absent from his mind. He had stopped ever feeling hungry or even peckish. He was simply going through the motions of discussing food, entertaining various options for dinner, possibly for my benefit. Soon he was eating half, and then less than half, of what I put in front of him.

'You haven't touched them,' I said when I re-entered the room minutes later. John stirred again at the sound of my accusation; he was always drowsy because of his medication.

'I'll just have the tea,' John said. He hadn't noticed the cup and saucer listing to one side on the breakfast tray, which had been tilted at an angle by the blue mattress undulating beneath him on his hospital bed.

'But John, you have to eat *something*,' I said, a hint of panic on the edge of my voice.

'If I don't want them I can't eat them,' he replied.

We might not have been experts about food and wine, but we had been enthusiastic amateurs with a shared commitment to regular practice. John's refusal of food was no hunger strike. His appetite had simply vanished. I tried not to let him see me cry as I left the bedroom.

~

Once I finally noticed John's sudden weight loss, it was all I could see. Drying his back after showering a few days later, I was shocked to see the outline of his shoulder blades protruding from his pale skin. There was no mistaking the thinness of an unhealthy body. John was *skeletal*. I asked casually if he had noticed losing any weight.

'No, I haven't,' he said. 'Have you?'

I retrieved one of our wedding photographs so he could compare his face as it was then with his face now. Was it only nine months ago? I wasn't sure this was a good idea, but John wanted to do it. Using the wheelchair, he was at sitting rather than standing height so he could no longer see himself in the bathroom mirror. I brought him a hand-held mirror. He held it up to his face to try to see the change in his appearance. He looked this way and that, holding the photograph in his other hand, comparing how he looked then with how he looked today. He continued to glance from one to the other, noting some increased definition in the bones of his face, but he didn't see any major difference.

John's self-perception was intriguing, because for me the contrast was now startlingly clear. His cheeks were sunken, which made his cheekbones seem overly prominent as a result. His jaw-line was sharp and angular rather than rounder and fleshed out. Metastases that appeared on his chest in recent months had grown markedly. He had dubbed the three that lined up vertically on his sternum 'the traffic lights'. His fine pale hands reminded me of a prima ballerina's. It was a relief that he couldn't see how dramatic the difference was.

~

John's condition had deteriorated so rapidly in the past three weeks that even we could no longer ignore the absurdity of my continuing to work — whether at the office, which had been happening less and less regularly in the previous couple of months as we oscillated between medical appointments and hospital; or from home, which I had until now been doing in short spurts of attention. His sudden decline was so evident that I organised with my employer to base myself at home for the remainder of the time John had left. Overnight it felt like we had weeks instead of months. How much time, exactly, no one could say, or if they could, they weren't prepared to tell us.

It was impossible to fathom how we had missed the signposts. It was as if John and I had been floating along a stream and had become inured to the incremental but increasing turbulence of the water. I had been thinking about hosting Christmas lunch at home that year for the first time. We regularly entertained my family and our friends because our home was the most comfortable venue for John. But Christmas was still months away. Until now I had not once doubted that John would be here to share it. We had failed to deduce the steep waterfall around the stream, just ahead of us.

Part Five

Homes of the Grave

25

A month or so after Catherine had parsed my home and devised a colour scheme that complemented my cool palette, Gerry and his gang of four started work. It was December, a few short weeks before my second Christmas without John. In 'The Burial of the Dead', the opening section of *The Wasteland*, T. S. Eliot writes that 'April is the cruellest month'. For me that dubious honour will always be a tie between October and November: October for the anniversary of John's death, and November for the anniversary of our wedding.

The walls were rendered by October, just shy of the first anniversary. I had been through a lot of *rinsing and repeating* by that stage. While my physical strength and mental stamina were back, I lacked any sense of a confident direction in which to head. Looking around me, every direction seemed still to end up at the same desolate place. No matter where I went, there I would be. And wherever I was, John was not. I dreaded the thought that struck me immobile in unexpected moments, that I would have to trudge through the years ahead by myself, knowing that I would never again feel John's arms around me, or see his smiling face welcoming me home.

~

Prior to the anniversary, I had been conscious of the date approaching and had valiantly determined just to take it as it comes. Despite projecting this brave face for myself, I had nevertheless anticipated a few tears. On the day, after spending time at John's grave and cleaning his headstone, which had become crusted with dust and mud from recent rain, I stayed close to home, filling in the hours by reading and playing the piano. In the evening a few close friends gathered to mark the anniversary with a meal. Hitting the pillow that night, I was a little chastened that the entire day had passed without my shedding so much as a single tear. Not even at the grave. All I felt was a sense of body-weariness and vague unease. I wondered if, like my house, I had simply dried out.

But just as my period has never arrived on time, so the physiological 'anniversary effect' did not fully kick in until a few days after the official date I had marked on my calendar in thick black pen: *One year today*. When it did, the body blow was so powerful I could barely propel myself forward. My physical movements were as stymied as if I had put on a straitjacket. A heavy fabric had wrapped around me invisibly but so tightly that my breathing felt constricted. I had never before felt so literally trapped in my own body. It was as if my body had its own physiological memory, which, now it was alert to the anniversary of John's death, had taken over all physical functions and shut down thought. My mind was held hostage, suspended and incapable of the smallest abstraction, while my body's internal clock *remembered* what had happened one year ago, if not precisely to the day. The date on my calendar had been a trigger for a related but separate chronology that my body, unbeknown to my rational mind, had been keeping.

Stuck in the mud of my mind, all I could think of to do to free myself was to try moving. Too dangerous to get behind the wheel of my car, I locked the house and set out on foot instead. In the end I wandered sluggishly for close to three hours around the neighbourhood John and I had shared, traversing the parks and paths in which we had walked, feeling numb and hyper-conscious all at once. The sun shone flagrantly, mocking my despair. Drifting, I felt like a yacht whose mast had been broken by a huge wave, a very long way from shore. At times I would physically come to a halt, stalled like a motor that suddenly petered out and refused to start again. When that happened I sat down on a park bench and stared without focusing into middle distance, oblivious to the squeals of children playing or the hum of distant traffic, my thoughts focused and not-focused at the same time.

My journal entry reflected the relentless din of questions in my head:

Here I am, back at the beginning. Again. Will this roller-coaster ever end? He is never coming back. How can I possibly continue living each day in my house, in Sydney, as if nothing has changed? Everything is different now. The city looks smaller. The people seem angrier. Each day is the same as the last. What am I going to do now, that will give me some sense of hope? A sense of direction?

The rendered walls served as an uneasy reminder of how far I had come, and the blank unwritten reality of my future path. However much I doubted my readiness, it was time to prepare the newly smooth surface for painting. To show the face of my house to the world.

~

The painters arrived armed with a truckload of equipment and Catherine's colour chart. These young men became part of my furniture for the six weeks it took them to prepare the walls and paint my house, inside and out. They studied the colour chart as if it were a map of foreign lands guiding them from room to room. They brought with them a paint-splattered old radio, cut lunches, and a sense of camaraderie. Growing up as the daughter of a builder, I always felt comfortable around these men and respected their lack of pretension. But they were shy with me. They didn't know quite what to make of a young woman living by herself in this grand old house. My external walls held up well under their casual scrutiny.

Exploring the superficial terrain of their working lives — discussing what the weather forecast meant for the job at hand, or whether they preferred cash or a cheque, for example — and hearing occasional snippets of their personal lives — the girlfriend, the mother-in-law — was like being a visitor in a new but strangely familiar territory. These conversations were no place for ideas or metaphor. I kept my symbolism to myself.

The painters had a lot of work to do before they could even begin playing with colour. First they had to scrape all traces of mould off the walls before washing them down with sugar soap. Then they filled the multitude of cracks and gaps in the walls not affected by rising damp, and smoothed out the unevenness in several of the ceilings. The young men clambered up and down scaffolding like so many Michelangelos, and dust flew in all directions as they sanded every surface to a fine finish.

The men fascinated me. I was charmed by their easy way with each other, joking around and ribbing one another, and envious of their long days of physical labour, which would exhaust them into nights of easy sleep. Highly conscious of the way they used their bodies, stretching upwards, bending down, moving quickly about the house, climbing ladders, shifting furniture and carrying tins of paint from one room to another. Taking their ability to do all of those things utterly for granted. Their experience of pain would be limited to a fuzzy recollection of a broken limb when they were children, an occasional stretched muscle, or a temporary bad back. Irrationally I felt moments of anger that they were not conscious of being free from pain. Why did John have to endure so much pain? Why was there so little I, or any of his doctors or nurses, could do to ease the burden that he had been forced to carry alone?

Daily life had resumed a barren predictability. I woke up, dressed, went to work, came home. But after six or seven months of this self-imposed pattern, I could no longer pretend that I was coping with my return to the office. I had too soon resumed the corporate routine, and could neither concentrate on my work in the office, or conduct the necessary forensic efforts in my domestic environment, without my mind racing. I asked my employer if I could move to working three days per week.

My employer thankfully granted my request, and within days of changing my working arrangements, I felt a visceral surge of relief. My time outside the office routine soon filled with its own patterns — the visits from contractors quoting on the job of painting the house, the visits to the accountant to file outstanding tax returns. My salary dropped, but for the first time my spirits lifted. I had taken a first step along my new path, even if I did not know where it would lead me.

26

As normal as possible, for as long as possible.

On an exquisite Saturday morning in early October, John and I were happily outside enjoying the sunshine and each other's company. The sky was a bright expanse of unfettered blue, the air was still buoyant with the last vestiges of spring. We congratulated ourselves on being up and out of the house much earlier than normal. It was still well before noon. Later I recalled reading accounts of the moments before the first hijacked plane crashed into the World Trade Center's North Tower, which had described the morning as perfect. Some days are just too good to be true.

That Saturday happened to be the day of the 2004 Australian Federal Election. It was John's first time voting in a Federal Election since he became a citizen in 2001. We made our way to the church hall at the top of our street to cast our ballots, then proceeded to our regular Saturday cafe. He watched me sip my cappuccino with the detached fascination of an anthropologist. He used to down one double-shot latte and immediately order another, and had lost the taste for coffee only recently. We chatted about nothing in particular.

'I'm feeling a bit breathless,' John said suddenly. 'Would you take me home now?'

Neither of us had paid much attention to John's recent bouts of breathlessness. They were brief, and seemed only to occur after

I had transferred him into or out of bed or the wheelchair. Despite my best efforts John still expended energy during each transfer, although now he was so much lighter to lift. I was concerned to hear him confess that he was out of breath, but assumed that being at home would help. At least we were only a few blocks away.

~

The answering machine indicated a new message, but I ignored its warning flash and pressed Play.

'John, it's Julie the palliative care nurse,' the recorded voice said brightly. 'We've just got your blood test results and your white blood cell count is . . . um, it's quite low, actually. We need you to come in for a blood transfusion. Would you call me as soon as you get this message?'

The news registered, but only faintly, as if it were intended for someone else. We were so weary of tests, nurses, doctors, syringes and pills, we shrugged off Julie's faintly plaintive tone and enjoyed a cup of tea on the back deck, watching the busy traffic of birds and insects and butterflies before reluctantly leaving for hospital. We were not ready to be cast out of our garden.

~

John's white blood cell count was so low, the doctor said, that he should not have been able to sit up in bed, let alone shower, get dressed, and vote as he had done that morning. At last we had an explanation for his pale complexion and breathlessness. Still, we assumed the blood transfusion would improve his condition sufficiently for us to return home, to our version of normal.

It was the first time that we found ourselves unexpectedly in Cassia Ward. Until today, John's hospitalisations had been known in advance, even if occasionally we had only a few days' notice. By this time we had honed our preparations for hospital to that of the frequent business traveller or heavily pregnant woman, who has an overnight bag packed with the essentials ready for the last-minute call to depart.

The palliative care ward of Canterbury Hospital had become a familiar environment to us by virtue of the frequency of John's hospitalisations in his final months, but it was the opposite of home. Even though there was more than enough 'hospital' inside our own home on a daily basis. Like public transport, or church, hospital was a place where it was impossible to feel *at* home.

So we brought home to the hospital instead. We arrived armed to combat the ward's systemic challenges to personality and identity with items carefully selected from home. Apart from some basic toiletries and a change of underwear, John liked to bring with him two books — always one fiction and one non-fiction; he liked Ian Rankin's crime novels and non-fiction works like Tim Flannery's *The Future Eaters* — in addition to the newspaper, some music to listen to, and his favourite photograph of us. It was a candid shot Sheila took late on the night of our wedding, after everyone else had left. In the photo I am grinning madly at the camera, my left arm around John to pull him close. He is leaning into me, his jacket off, tie askew, beaming.

The nurses in the palliative care ward didn't mind us cracking open a bottle of wine, or my bringing in some Japanese food for John instead of the hospital's bland fare. What harm would a glass of wine or some contraband ice cream present? Cassia Ward was this hospital's death row, and John its youngest inmate by decades.

It is said that a day is a long time in politics. It can be a long time in hospital too. By the time John had been admitted and seen by a doctor, voting had stopped and the counting and television commentary had begun. Something else had started, too: although John had admitted himself under his own weak steam only hours earlier, he now required a tube to help him to breathe. John was hooked up to the transfusion machine and also to a ventilation machine, which through a thin tube with plastic tines passed oxygen into his nostrils. A tussle for supremacy began between the curved ends of the thin breathing tube, which were supposed to fit around each ear, and John's glasses, which until this moment had perched comfortably in the same places. The tube's nostril forks were its secret weapon in the battle: they were able to induce nosebleeds just to add to the variety of John's distress.

Within a few hours of John's admission he developed waves of pain in his stomach that the nurses suspected indicated a bowel obstruction. Constipation, a uniform and frustrating side-effect of most of his medication, had worsened significantly over the past week. John writhed in agony, his breathing difficulties exacerbated by the intense abdominal pain. The doctor explained they could not treat his bowel obstruction until the blood transfusion was complete.

The envelope-sized television above John's bed was tuned to the ABC's election coverage, but he paid fleeting attention to the screen above him. The world outside this hospital room was on seven-second delay. In front of me my husband was dying. In real time. I was immobilised by the fear, felt for the first time, that this night might be his last. I could barely see for the tears streaming down my cheeks. Hours passed. I held my world by the hand, too terrified to let go. The nurses kindly worked around me. John could not speak, he was so short of breath; we kept upping the oxygen in his tube, only to find out from one of the nurses that it was up too high. Distrustful, we watched her turn it back down and administer a muscle-relaxing pill under John's tongue instead. I was anxious that the pill wouldn't work, anxious about how quickly it might take to work, anxious that John be more comfortable. There was nothing I could do except be anxious, which was of no use to anyone. Thankfully the muscle relaxant helped him settle into a half-sleep, and his breathing slowly became less laboured.

Somehow we were granted a new day, and the blood transfusion dripped away like water on sandstone. His body was shutting down, and not being able to expel any of his own body's waste was a sure sign that he was now lying in his deathbed. But John seemed unaware of how the local issue of his constipation related to the bigger picture of his rapidly deteriorating health.

'Any progress, darling?' I inquired on our third day in the hospital. His transfusion was complete and the doctors' attention had turned to treating the bowel obstruction. He was sufficiently stable that I could make a quick trip home to procure supplies.

'Not a sausage, Pumpkin,' he said. Then, after catching his breath, 'Feels like I've got a . . . a fucking concrete cork up the chuff.' He remained confident that his bottom would behave, eventually. 'When this thing blows, I hope they've got their helmets cemented on,' he declared breathlessly later that day. I burst out laughing.

Each night I camped beside John on a fold-out bed. I watched him as he breathed, and as he slept, and stayed awake willing the sun to come up. At four or five in the morning, as confident as I could be that he had made it through to the new morning, I would collapse into a deep sleep, only to wake two hours later to the stern instruction of the nurse on duty to get up and fold my bed out of his way. Mine was a redundant presence to everyone except John.

~

The next day while I was buying coffee in the hospital cafeteria the doctor had been in to see John. She came to tell him about the results of scans they had taken of his abdomen and lungs the previous afternoon. The tumour's growth had distorted the shape of his bowel and bladder, radically inhibiting its normal functioning. She also reported a one-third increase in disease in his lungs.

John realised for the first time how little time he had left. I bounced into the patients' dining room about ten minutes after the doctor left John. He confessed later that, seeing me smiling at him, he didn't know how he was going to tell me what he'd just learned.

'I might not even have six weeks,' he said.

Six weeks! It was a small relief for me that he did not suspect he had so little time left. Six *days* felt like a lifetime to me at that moment. *If only we had six weeks*, I thought.

Our new knowledge had two immediate effects. First, within an hour the Constipation Crisis was over. And over everything. Second, whether by coincidence or design, John was the most clear-headed he had been since arriving in hospital. It was time for us to talk.

~

The setting for what would be our final conversation took place amid plastic pot-plants, dog-eared paperback editions of Leon Uris and Wilbur Smith novels, a large round beige table with matching chairs, a tapestry of dubious artistic merit — a gift from a former patient's family that prompted hallucinations in John later in the day — and, of all things, a small Casio keyboard. In hindsight, there was something peculiarly appropriate about the blandness of the patients' dining room for the highly charged exchange that occurred there. Its generic décor provided no distraction from the proper focus of the scene that played out there between us that afternoon. It was no scene that I had ever imagined, let alone witnessed on television. I was one of its two leading characters, but we had no script to guide us. There had been so little dialogue in the past few days. We smiled at each other, held hands, and improvised.

Later I tried to recapture what each of us said to the other, desperate to record his exact words and my fumbling speech forever. All I could do, in the hours and weeks that followed this extraordinary two hours, was piece together scraps and fragments of our conversation as they recurred to me.

'I am so happy that we married, darling,' I said. 'I hope you know how much I've loved our life together.'

'I'm so delighted you said yes!' John replied. Even now, the way he said it betrayed his enduring surprise that it ever happened. 'It was effortless being together.' He paused at regular intervals to catch his breath, but he was lucid.

'I am so proud to be your wife. It is an honour to be your wife. I love you so much.' I laughed and cried at the same time, refusing to believe he wouldn't be here soon to hear me trying these words again, in an attempt to get them to actually convey what I meant. 'You showed me how to be part of a team.'

'You picked it up so quickly!' he said, as if it had been the easiest thing in the world for me to do. 'I love you very much, Virginia. You have made me very happy,' he said.

We gripped each other and held on for dear life.

'I know the first months will be hard. The hardest thing you've ever had to do,' he said. 'But I don't want you to dwell on the past. Remember all our wonderful moments and laughs and how we made the most of the time we had. Take it with you. It will carry you forward into your future. I want you to live a full and rich life, for both of us. I don't want you to get bogged down wallowing in grief.'

My chest felt as if it were caving in from the pressure on it. I shook my head as the tears welled up again. 'But how am I supposed to go on? How am I going to live without you? What do you expect me to do?'

'I want you to live for the both of us — I want you to have a rich and full life,' he said again.

'But how am I going to make you proud of me, darling?' I wept, clinging to him like driftwood even as I knew I was drowning.

'I want to say something to you,' he said suddenly, with a sense of urgency. 'I want you to marry again. You're young. Have a child if you can — the child that you and I couldn't have.'

How did he manage such clarity? We had decided on Finn

and Alice as the names for the children we would never have, but the discussion had always been theoretical.

'Don't put me on a pedestal,' he said. 'I don't want you to compare all men to me.' He never regarded himself as highly as I did, but he knew he was a good husband. To think, when we first met, I was afraid that he would want to place me on a pedestal.

'No one could ever take your place,' I said, wiping away his tears as well as my own.

'I don't want them to take my place — but I want you to live for us both. Promise me you will do that.'

'I promise, darling. I promise I'll try.'

I don't know if John felt it, but I experienced a feeling of completion and serenity during our talk that day. A temporary peace, like that in the eye of a hurricane. Miraculously we were not once disturbed in the two or so hours that we spent among the vinyl and plastic. We felt privileged to be able to have that conversation — celebrating what we had shared, and to say everything we wanted to say to each other — when many couples' lives are destroyed by an accident. We could prepare — to the extent that it was possible — to say goodbye to each other, knowing our life together was about to end.

John must have felt some inexorable change within himself, because he charged me with specific tasks: to call his brother, David, in England, and Sheila in Ireland; to purchase a thank-you gift for the nurses on the ward; and to make sure to give his watch to Robert, his nephew. Then he dictated the message that he asked me to share with his friends. He didn't hesitate once as to what he wanted to say. It took him a while to get the words out, but his measured delivery made me suspect he had composed them some time ago.

I wrote them down as if I were an emissary from another land, bringing back the last wishes of a prince mortally wounded on a battlefield. John was relying on me to take the words down carefully, and to see that the message got through to his beloved troops. I repeated them word for word in the message that I sent out in the hours after his death.

As for funeral arrangements, all I could confirm was that John expected to be buried rather than cremated. Even then the last thing I wanted to do while he was still drawing breath was talk about a time when he wasn't.

'Are you afraid of dying?' I asked him at one point.

'Not really,' he replied. 'I just don't know what lays over there,' tilting his head slightly in the direction of the great unknown. He paused and looked at me sheepishly. 'That's not a very Catholic thing to say, is it?'

John was not a religious man. He described himself as a 'cultural Catholic'. He found the weekly mass a meditative and quiet space for contemplation, although he had stopped attending services when his mobility declined. He felt a sense of community at the church, too, especially during the years he lived on his own. But that wasn't to say he believed much of what he heard there.

He'd often come home, where I'd be playing the piano, to tick off the priest. 'That man is such a fucking homophobe,' he'd say, shaking his head. 'Play *Autumn Leaves* for me.' Still, in the two weeks before entering hospital for the last time, the priest twice visited John at home for private conversations, and he had taken communion since entering the palliative care ward.

That night, John asked me to play something for him on the banged-up Casio keyboard. The October air was stifling. It was difficult to know where the coolest place in the ward at any given time might be. We had moved John, hospital bed and all, into the dining room once more. My heart soared that I could do something new that would give him pleasure at this eleventh hour.

When asked for a request he didn't hesitate. 'Strangers in the Night,' he gasped. I wondered if he remembered us singing along to Frank Sinatra's version in the car driving home from Mudgee, a wine-growing district four hours from Sydney, where we had spent a long weekend with friends. It was hard to believe the trip had been little more than one year ago. Cringing at the poor quality of the keyboard's plastic sound, I picked out the tune as accurately as I could and added some basic chords with my left hand. My fingers slipped off the narrow keys in the humidity. John seemed pleased by it, and I was seized by regret that I had not played for him more often at home. At one point I turned to him and reminded him of the part where Sinatra scats one entire chorus: 'doo-be doo-be doo, be-doo be-doo bu . . .' He smiled, but said nothing. At the end of the song, I looked up and realised that John wanted to be wheeled back to the relative cool of the ward. One song was all he needed. My brief set was over.

Later that night as I changed into a t-shirt to sleep in, I leaned across to give him a kiss before hopping into the camp bed. John, who had been increasingly silent and still, reached out his hands and gave my breasts a good squeeze. I jumped in surprise and started giggling. He just raised his eyebrows and gave me a cheeky smile. He could no longer speak or breathe unassisted, but his desire was as strong as ever.

There was something about John's last day that took on an epic quality, so that in my mind's eye it seems to have lasted an age. During the day he received a procession of visitors, who each stared into his placid eyes with a mixture of fear, admiration and wonder. Some crumbled at the sight of him so physically diminished, but saved their tears for outside his room. One friend brought in her six-month-old daughter, who reached out her chubby pink fist to touch John's thin forearm, pale as petrified wood. 'New life,' he said quietly, smiling into her eyes.

John gave the nurses lip to the last. The Malaysian nurse who talked a lot explained that she had lost her voice. John took a gulp of oxygen and said faintly, 'I bet your family is disappointed.'

Of all our friends and colleagues who saw John that day, only one knew for certain he would never see John again. Michael was flying to Melbourne to sit for an examination that was the final step in his qualifying as a specialist obstetrician-gynecologist. He came to the hospital en route to the airport.

Standing in front of John, Michael told him where he was going, and asked John to wish him luck. He leaned towards John to give him a hug.

'Whatever luck I have left, mate, it's yours,' John replied immediately, hardly able to get the words out. Michael bolted upright, tears in his eyes.

~

As the late afternoon drew into early evening, I felt some irrevocable change taking place. From our sterile prison I watched the last of the day's sun burn from pink to a dark and angry orange before it dipped below the horizon. Turning excitedly to John to see if he had noticed it too, he no longer seemed to be aware of anything further afield than the borders of his hospital bed.

One of the nurses who cared enough to be honest with me, said, 'Don't be surprised if he doesn't make it through tonight.' His words reinforced what I knew in the pit of my stomach. There was nothing else to do but to sit beside him in his hospital bed and feel the universe shifting gear.

I kept talking to John as he gradually adopted the fixed

middle-distance gaze of semi-consciousness. I told him I'd finally arranged everything for us to go home the next day. 'Don't let me die here,' he had said to me, urgently, when he realised time was running out. 'Promise me you won't let me die here!' I tried my best to get him home. We wanted so much to return there together, to be surrounded by the things we love, the comforts that only home can provide. He liked my idea of setting him up in his hospital bed in the living room, so he would be centrally located to all the activities of the house: we talked about how he could receive visitors, watch his large-screen television, listen to me come and go from the kitchen or play the piano in the hallway. But we lost two days in getting his blood transfusions, and the nurses couldn't help his bowel to work with medication until after the transfusion was complete. In order to get him home, canisters of oxygen needed to be organised first. Finally we had secured oxygen and delivery for the morning. Logistically speaking, we could go home together. But it was all theoretical now.

I desperately hoped that the prospect of being home again would be sufficient to keep him alive another day.

'Please don't go, darling,' I wept, then retracted my words at the sight of his body, finally defeated. 'I'm just being selfish. If you have to go, I understand. I don't want you to go, but I know you have to.'

He squeezed my hand or my thumb every so often to let me know he could still hear me as I talked.

My arms grew sore, leaning against the rails of the hospital bed. Nurses came and went. I don't know how much time passed. But at some point I was struck by the knowledge that John was no longer in any pain. I cannot recall how I knew; the recognition was pure instinct. Paradoxically, the fact he was slipping further away presented us with one last opportunity. There was one more thing I could do for both of us, something that we had longed to do for such a long time and had not been able to.

I climbed over the rails of the hospital bed and lay the full length of my body against his. John and I were lying together again, as husband and wife.

As normal as possible, for as long as possible.

Here was the body I loved, the body that had been forced to accommodate desire and disease at once, free from pain at last. John knew exactly where I was. His hand gave mine a light squeeze as I settled in alongside him in the narrow bed. He knew we were lying together, finally, one last time. I clung to him as he lay close to death, as I could not when he was nearer to life. I cradled him in my arms. I ran my hand through his beautiful soft curly hair, and caressed his belly, his arms, his legs. Sometimes I talked to him, and he gently squeezed my hand in response.

A few hours must have gone by. At one point I was mortified to have to get up to visit the toilet. For a few minutes I debated whether or not to go. If I left it any longer, he would only be closer to death. The idea of relieving myself, of being *on the toilet*, at the moment John died, was impossible to contemplate, and it was this that motivated me up off the hospital bed. Having to shift his body in order to move, I was surprised at how heavy he was against me. I was disgusted at my healthy system; that it continued to function without the slightest regard for what else might be happening around it. Life was reduced to its most basic urges and commands: breathing, pissing, sleeping, dying. Returning to the hospital bed, John seemed even heavier and less aware of my presence as I settled back in beside him.

Some time later one of the nurses came into the room to check on his breathing and, seeing us in the bed together, left quickly. I appreciated her leaving us alone to enjoy the precious but compromised intimacy that was still available to us. Finite, final moments that we could share. John's breathing had gradually become more regular, but it sounded shallow. His pulse had slowed although I did not know it. It seemed like hours since the last time he had gently squeezed my hand.

There was no point watching the clock. But at some point in the early hours of a Thursday morning in October, life stood still: two loud breaths, about five seconds apart. I hope never to hear an inhalation like it again; his short, dreadful rasp that swallowed the air and time along with it. Its sound was quite distinct from all the breaths that had preceded it, as if John were filling his sails to set out on this final voyage. There was no doubting that this was the sound of his last breath, but still it took long seconds for me to draw the logical, inconceivable conclusion. I knew, but could not quite believe, that he was dead. I didn't scream or wail, I just started crying quietly and held on to my husband, hugging him close.

My love. My life. My lighthouse.

A passing nurse heard me make what must be, for those whose ears are attuned to it, an unmistakable sound. She entered our curtained-off room, took one look at me, and checked John's pulse. 'Darling, oh no . . . is he . . . oh yes, he's gone. I'm sorry, love.'

Somewhere, as if at the end of a very dark, empty corridor, I heard a door close with a soft, irrevocable thud.

27

I breathed and John did not. Slumped in the back of my parents' car, I kept breathing as they drove me away from John, away from the hospital where he had died two hours earlier. They had come to collect me, to take me home. Wherever home was now. It was about four o'clock in the morning. We walked in the front door and sat quietly on the couch. I remember that Mum made us a cup of tea and that I sat completely still. Not moving, barely breathing. I'm not sure I was fully conscious. Part of me had died. You can't be a little bit pregnant, but you can be a little bit dead. My parents, thankfully, knew there was nothing to say. At some point Dad suggested I try to get some sleep. He had to help me to stand up from the couch where I had been sitting. My legs couldn't quite manage the task on their own. I remember it was light outside. He put me into my single bed, just as he had done when I was a little girl. Only I wasn't a little girl. I was thirty-four years old, a married woman, and this single bed had been mine now for months. I turned my back to the empty height-adjustable bed John had been forced to use, the hospital bed that changed the configuration and the function of our bedroom. I didn't know what to do. Look out the window at the beginning of the new day, the first of a world without John in it? Shut my eyes? Whether my eyes were open or closed, I saw the same thing. Our final scene. Over and over.

A few hours later I rang my dear friend Jen and she came over immediately. Even though she'd seen John yesterday in hospital, emaciated and breathing through a tube, she was shocked at the news. He'd hung valiantly in his corner, fighting for every last available breath in those lungs riddled with tumour. Still, nobody expected him to actually *die*. My brother brought his three-year-old son with him. He ran in the yard and watched the planes fly low overhead on their descent towards Sydney Airport. I envied his obliviousness. Mum and Dad sat glued to their seats, grief-stricken for their daughter and beloved son-in-law. We all sat around the table out the back under the leaking awning, sipping tea.

I remember a feeling of being stunned. Winded. Like I had been operated on to remove all my organs and abandoned mid-procedure, sedated and hyper-conscious at the same time. I stared blankly, unfocused, as my friends and family talked. They appeared to need a sign from me that indicated I was functioning. I made sounds that formed words that formed sentences. It seemed to help.

It took me a while to realise I was now what people call a *widow*.

~

About six weeks after John's funeral I flew to the UK and Ireland to attend memorial services for John that Sheila had arranged. The flight to London was enjoyable for the fact that it was a vacuum. I drank wine and tried to read, but found it impossible to concentrate.

Then I tried watching a film. I had never realised how profoundly self-centred grief was. But every story was about us, everything I saw somehow reminded me of John. A garden-variety crime thriller brought me undone by the pointless death of a child; an animated movie made my eyes well up through its ability to manipulate my already taut heart strings. And anything remotely to do with love was completely unwatchable. I tried once or twice on the flight, but I started sobbing, shoulders heaving with the effort of containing the tears, controlling my running nose, and doing all of that without making a noise much above a whimper. My personal drama went unnoticed, except perhaps by the only other person not to be asleep during the cabin's enforced blanket of night. Even with the chemical encouragement of a pill and several glasses of wine, there was no sleep.

On the date of what would have been our first wedding anniversary, I was in London. I had, the day before, attended a memorial service for my late husband. The memorial service was an opportunity for John's friends and family to gather and mourn for their brother, their colleague, their friend. It was held at the Gospel Oak church John had spent a lot of time in growing up. A few days later I flew to Ireland and did it all over again, this time with John's cousins and other family members whom I had met once before only fifteen months earlier, on our honeymoon.

What was I thinking? Certainly I had not imagined the well-meaning embraces of strangers, the hospitality of John's cousins and the excessive quantities of prepared food, the endless headache, the lonely minutes waiting for each polite conversation to present a gap in it so I could escape. Neither did I anticipate John's cousin, the assistant priest for John's memorial in the Irish country village, calling me 'the widow Victoria' throughout the service. I wondered briefly if he needed to distinguish me from some other widow of John's who had been part of another service earlier that day.

More than one hundred people attended the London service — not bad for a young man who had left the old country behind nine years earlier when he emigrated to Australia. I could tell John's extended family and old friends were admiring my brave face; they had no inkling that the John they were remembering was someone else from the husband I mourned.

There was no doubt in my mind that I would attend the memorial service. None of my friends or my family questioned my decision. If they had, I would have gone anyway. At the time it didn't strike me as unusual or too much. In retrospect it seems inconceivable that I undertook this journey — in my journal I described it as a *pilgrimage* — on my own. It was six weeks after John's death. But I did not think of myself as being alone. Not yet. I was daunted but quietly thrilled at the prospect of seeing lots of people who knew and loved John. I hoped that being surrounded by his friends, family and former colleagues would buoy me. This trip was a way for me to keep John alive.

Our wedding anniversary, 29 November, was the day after the memorial service in London. My hosts — John's dearest friend, Maria, whom I had come to love as my own friend, and her mother, at whose home I was staying — were concerned at my spending this, of all days, alone. I couldn't explain to them that I didn't feel alone. They finally agreed on the condition that we would all have dinner together that evening.

Of all the countless ways in which I could have spent this day, my choices were telling. I could have had a facial and a massage, or wandered through Selfridges with my credit card. I could have bought myself a ticket to a West End show. But the first stop on my wedding anniversary tour was the Tower of London.

Joining a guided tour meant I didn't have to wonder about where I should walk or what to do next. I just followed the man at the front of our group. I shuffled mindlessly through the walled fortifications and became lost in the gruesome chronology of the place. I relished standing close to the very spot where Anne Boleyn and Catherine Howard were beheaded by their husband, Henry VIII. I was morbidly spellbound by the stories of imprisonments and executions. Like an autistic person who feels calmer when heavy pressure is applied, squeezing them, I felt better with the weight of history bearing down on my own personal trauma. Somehow it helped me to put my loss into the broader perspective of history and chronology. I could choose not to take personally the gross unfairness and sheer randomness of John's disease. The Tower was proof that human history is a catalogue of unfairness, randomness, too-early death. If life is cruel to everyone, in one way or another, then how could I stand outside the tide of history and continue to feel that I had been personally wronged?

I tried so hard on this day to convince myself that losing him wasn't momentous. I willed myself to remember that I was fortunate in the *love and support* of my parents and close friends; that I had an interesting and well-paid job to go home to, with a *network* of professional colleagues; that I had *means* at my disposal. That my life had an infrastructure, and an architecture, to it; that I was not staring into an *abyss*. My mind worked overtime to devise ways for me to consider that my loss was not devastating, that my life had not just fallen apart and changed forever. Thinking about Anne and Catherine, I couldn't help but envy them a little for losing their heads.

But beheadings and royal intrigue were not enough. I needed to dwell and tarry longer among the dead. So I took the tube to the Imperial War Museum. I was pleasantly surprised by the peacefulness of an institution dedicated to warfare. A respectful silence reigned. Best of all, I was completely anonymous. No one knew who I was, or why I was there on this particular day, or at all. I had found a vacuum in which to exist for a few hours. I could be alone with my thoughts. Alone with John.

I wandered through the comprehensive exhibits of the two World Wars. The re-creations of the trenches from these conflicts were especially compelling. I spent quite a while pondering all that cold packed earth. All those lives that had been protected, saved, and lost, beneath ground level. The daily fight to survive. The bureaucracy that managed to establish itself in subterranean clay offices. The personal touches that made the trench a surreal respite of sorts for the young men who were flung into each other's company far from home — a hair comb, a crumpled paper with handwritten lyrics to a popular song, a photograph of a girlfriend smudged by dirt-stained fingers.

Together John and I had watched many World War II films and documentaries. He loved military history. One of his favourite films was *The Dam Busters*. He always made me laugh with his impersonation of the pilots who bombed the dams of the Ruhr and subsequently made their way into World War II legend. The film's theme music has a rousing chorus that John would hum while twisting his arms up and back so that he could join his thumbs and forefingers, press them against his eyes, in imitation of the aviator glasses the pilots wore. He also liked to make me laugh by yelling one of the film's catch-phrases, 'Chocks away, Ginger!', in the plummiest possible accent when he had been successful in the bathroom, like his pilot heroes did when dropping a bomb.

Months later I found a collection of small illustrated books from his boyhood in which he had carefully pasted pictures of fighter planes collected out of a weekly series in one of the London newspapers. Decades on, they were in pristine condition. I was so moved by the fact he had kept them all these years.

The main attraction at the Imperial War Museum at the time of my visit was its highly regarded Holocaust exhibition. I wandered from room to room, drunk with death. I stood transfixed in front of a display of hundreds of pairs of discarded shoes collected at a death camp, which were encased in two floor-to-ceiling sheets of Perspex that ran along the entire length of one room. I examined the scale-model of Bergen-Belsen complete with railway tracks and tiny human figures, and felt irrational irritation when anyone else came into the room. Here was death on an unimaginable scale, in a most unsentimental presentation. The displays and personal stories in this exhibition did for me what nothing else could — put one life and one death into perspective, however briefly. John and I might have been robbed of time together, but he wasn't murdered. He did not choose to die, but neither did anybody else make that choice for him.

~

Returning to my empty house a few days later was a sobering experience. It had been empty when I left for London ten days earlier, but this time the emptiness screamed its welcome. Arriving home marked with finality the end of all formal ceremonies and celebrations of John's life. There would be no further occasions for which I would liaise with others over details and focus on John as the centre and purpose of the event. People had gathered for his funeral, his London memorial service, and for his mass in Ireland. But now there were no more events to plan for or look forward to. The formal part of the program had officially drawn to a close. What role was there for me to play now? I was a widow on an empty stage. My next role was one I would have to write myself.

28

The need to buy a work of art gripped me in those first harrowing weeks. Fortunately, a photograph found me and demanded that I buy it. The photograph, by Bill Henson, was large and imposing and difficult to ignore. Measuring 127 centimetres high by 180 centimetres wide, it depicts a rickety white wooden bridge over a shallow running stream, in which the stream disappears around a bend at the top right-hand corner of the picture, into an unidentified source of intense light. The little wooden bridge is lit in such a way that it stands out eerily pale against the exquisite palette of deep night reflected in the water flowing underneath it. Quietly pulsating with life in the midst of a rich and complex darkness, the bridge is gently embraced by the source of light, which the viewer cannot see but whose effects are undeniable. Seeing the photograph for the first time, on the website of the gallery that represents the photographer, I was transfixed. Henson's photographs had always moved me, but none of them had affected me as forcefully as this one.

In the silent tumult of my despair, one idea had become fixed: that some abstract representation of my loss — John was just around that corner, where the light was, I knew it — would help assuage the actual loss I could not deny. A creative work would gesture towards a place beyond physical pain and suffering, a realm beyond the immediate signals of my own distress. The power of symbols would assert their ineffability and render my grief, at least partially, into submission. The work would stay with me, to help me mark the time that is past and the transition to the unknowable future.

A well-meaning friend had lent me a series of *Women's Weekly*-style 'User Guides to Grief'. The pastel-coloured booklets all chorused, Don't make any changes. Don't throw out all of your clothes or buy a complete new wardrobe. Don't sell your house. Don't quit your job. Don't cut all your hair off or dye it a radically different colour. *Don't. Do. Anything*. This was not what I wanted to hear. Scouring these simplistic texts for the least scrap of useful advice, I noticed they said nothing about buying a work of art.

Why, then, a photograph? Why not a painting, a sculpture, an illustration? Perhaps it was the photograph's ability, however artificially, to speak at once of a fleeting moment and of permanence that attracted me most; the sense of a single moment in time arrested and, from that moment, suspended beyond time. No matter what happens for the rest of my life, this photograph will always look the same. It will not change. It will not leave me. It will not die.

The photograph's subject — the rickety white bridge over turbulent water, encased in the dark blanket of night — was the most compelling factor in my decision to buy it. Bridges have always functioned as a motif in my life. I grew up on Sydney's lower North Shore, gazing at the Tarban Creek Bridge and the approach to Gladesville Bridge from where I sat at my piano, for at least one hour every day from the age of seven. While perched on the piano stool, practising my scales and arpeggios, falling in love with Bach's *Preludes and Fugues*, or picking out by ear melodies from my father's collection of Frank Sinatra and Ella Fitzgerald recordings, I watched the cars and trucks flow over the bridges into and out of the city, and the sailboats and dinghies flow under them. The bridges carried people across them in those vehicles, and guarded the people who sailed beneath them. I watched as they brought people closer together. There was a palpable sense of life — I could see the evidence of it every time I sat at the piano — but it remained safely out of reach, behind the glass. As I turned ever more sharply inward during my adolescence, isolated and sometimes ostracised at school for being able to sight-read music and thereby becoming the school's ever-reliable — sole — accompanist, the piano by the window at home became my safe haven. The bridges spoke of a connection to other people that I envied but did not know; admired but could not feel.

A bridge appeared once again during my graduate work at the University of Sydney, although it took me some time to notice it. The research for my doctoral dissertation on the generation of American poets born in 1899 ballooned until I could no longer find a productive and — critically for a PhD — unique entry point. 'The Brooklyn Bridge keeps making an appearance,' my supervisor remarked of one early draft chapter. 'Why don't you try focusing on that?' The bridge became my key. Four years later, I submitted my dissertation on the battle between words and images in the poetry of Hart Crane, focused on his use of the Brooklyn Bridge in his major work, *The Bridge*.

Bridges are as metaphorical as they are literal. Buying the photograph of the little white bridge felt extravagant, but it made sense. I needed its symbolism as much as its beauty. I could ignore the picture as easily as I could forget it. It didn't matter that I would be digging a massive hole in my savings to buy it. I held someone else's nerve, if not my own, and put down a deposit.

~

When I had paid the final instalment on the photograph and it had been framed and hung, I had been widowed for about eight months. Friends came by to pay their respects to the massive work, which looked completely at home on my living room wall. Ultimately the acquisition had been a hopeful act, although at the time it was impossible for me to grasp it as such. These days, when I look closely at the photograph, I feel proud. Proud of myself for not letting self-doubt get in the way of my decision to buy it, even though I burnt a hole in my pocket as a result. Proud of having put such a dramatic stamp on the home I made with John. The photograph serves as a powerful and enduring reference to the tectonic change in my life which inspired its purchase, and to the conscious and unconscious kinds of improvement I was making.

Part Six

My Home, My Self

29

The garden between the house and the street was the one outstanding piece of my renovation puzzle. The multiple transformations of my domestic space to now had been contained within my home's three exterior walls. While these initially structural and subsequently cosmetic changes had been taking place, the front garden's high hedges, which separated the shallow square of lawn from the street front, had proved to be a silent bastion of support.

Conspiring with the hedge to increase my seclusion was the thick vine of Chinese jasmine thriving above the face of the wide porch that greeted visitors to the house. The vine, encouraged by regular pruning, had spread across the entire width of the house along a wooden lattice. Over the years it had crept upwards from its two bases at the foot of the columns on either side of the steps to the front porch, whose roof the columns supported. The vine's luxuriant dark green foliage sheltered the front of the house from sunlight and the gaze of passers-by. For a few weeks every year, in what roughly passes for spring in Sydney, the vine burst into a riot of white fragrant blossoms, their heady aroma apparent as soon as you arrived at the front gate. The slightest breeze sent blossoms tumbling to the ground, but there were always so many more where they had come from. In keeping with its sweet, brief season, as soon as the jasmine flourished, it was gone, leaving in its wake a carpet of wilted drying blossoms wherever the wind scattered them.

My decision to cut back the hedge took even me by surprise. Possibly the lengthy process of renovation had made me impatient to dramatise its finale: the painters' work had visibly transformed my house and I wanted everyone to see it. There was no longer any reason to shield it behind a tall thick hedge. In recent months it had become clear that the hedge was towering disproportionately over the garden, and it was time for some tough love. Instead of straddling the front fence from a great height, as it now did, the hedge would be levelled to the same height as the fence, and its leaves henceforth kept a manicured inch or two away. If the trim was too severe the hedge could always grow back, I thought, as if I were rationalising a bad haircut.

More audacious was my decision to remove the crowded vines from across the front of the house, and to bring down the wooden trellis that had held them up for so many years. Torn down in the name of home improvement, lying sprawled and defeated on the grass, they reminded me of those strings of Christmas lights that, at some indefinable point in the week or so after Christmas Day, turn from a source of nostalgic delight to an embarrassment that must be hurriedly dismantled and forgotten. I felt bad for the vines. Tipping my hat to past and future, I left the roots of the vine in the soil in the hope that a new vine, made stronger by surviving its near-destruction, would emerge and thrive in the years to come.

The effects of my kamikaze gardening were suitably violent. The entire frontage of my house was now exposed for the world to see. Strangers on their way past the house stopped at the gate and stared in amazement. Cars slowed down so their drivers could take in the garden's savage transformation. The dark green trench coat my house had been wearing had been yanked wide open. I might as well have been standing there stark naked myself. Light streamed into my bedroom window, unimpeded by the thick vines that only yesterday had hindered its passage. From the bedroom I looked out at my garden. All that remained of the hedge was a connected maze of twigs and branches. The hedge looked bereft without its leaves, like a lamb that had been shorn for the first time. I half-expected someone to scoop up the bald twigs in his arms and cart them away somewhere to start a fire. To kindle them with kindness in a home more welcoming than the garden in which they now stood, naked and vulnerable, blinking at the daylight.

30

At my farewell, which began in the afternoon to accommodate those friends with children, the last guest didn't leave until after midnight. There had only been one possible venue for this party, and I was fortunate there were many people who wanted to celebrate with me. Friends I had not seen in some time wandered through the house, astounded at the freshly painted walls and the near-empty rooms. 'I never realised the house had so much character,' one said to me. 'All these details, brought to life by paint. Who would have thought?'

In a few days I would be leaving Sydney for a new life in New York. I had resigned from the law firm I had worked for over the past six years, to the great surprise of everyone except my immediate colleagues, and rented out the house to trustworthy tenants. The house was packed up. After jettisoning so many household items and pieces of furniture over the past eighteen months, it was only partly furnished. The spare room was crammed full of boxes of books, CDs and DVDs, the contents of my kitchen, bottles of red wine that would hopefully age well, and the washing machine that would not cope with the demands of the tenants' growing family.

I had thought carefully about what, of the accumulated things I had not discarded during those long months of domestic frenzy, I actually needed to take with me. There wasn't much that could be described as essential: my clothes; a portable hard disk with all my documents and photographs on it; framed photographs of me and John — at home, on our wedding day — and the iPod my parents had bought me as a farewell gift. Less critical but also included were volumes of plays and memoirs, my current reading. I could buy these books in New York, I knew, but preferred to keep them close, like good friends.

I had asked John, at the very end, whether it would be all right with him if I tried to write about us. He just looked at me askance and said dismissively, 'Not much of a story is it.' There wasn't even a question mark at the end of his sentence. But during the past year I had suddenly written a short play about my clumsy efforts to find the words to put on his headstone. It was my first attempt at writing something that was not primarily an academic or commercial exercise; or for my eyes only, like a journal entry. Friends and family were uniformly encouraging. Nobody but me seemed surprised that I had tried to write a play. I submitted it to a festival of short plays, where it made it into the 'long-list' but progressed no further. Still, I was shocked and thrilled that my play had registered, however faintly, on the judges' radar. Perhaps I wasn't entirely out of my mind, months later, to be thinking about writing down some of my experiences as a young widow.

But one thing was clear: if I was going to try to write, I could not do it in the house where so much of the action had taken place. The decision to leave Sydney had crept up slowly, but, once reached, my mind was made up. Gradually over the horizon I had seen a vision of my immediate future. One more change — a change of scene — might be one I actually needed. John had been right to insist that I keep open the option of utilising my green card. I had the right to live and work in the USA and, finally, it felt like the right time to exercise it. It was a relief to acknowledge that I wanted to leave the city I had called home my entire life. Never would there be a more opportune moment to try living somewhere else. I booked a ticket from Sydney to New York City for the last day of March 2006. By then it would be almost eighteen months since John died. One more momentous change, to cap all the changes I had endured in the short years to this moment. But at least this change was one that I elected. A change that I embraced. The certainty with which I felt the desire to leave was refreshing. I had felt so little certainty about most things during the past year. Suddenly it made perfect sense for me to move to New York.

~

During the first week in New York I would be staying with the friend who had hosted me when I made the dash to extend my green card just under two years earlier. My sole task that week would be to find a place to call my own. I needed light and space, and neither of those things would be easy to find, let alone afford. Hours of scrolling through the Craig's List website had provided a crash-course in the price of Manhattan accommodation. Suddenly it was clear why two unrelated strangers shared a studio apartment, or sub-let a living room as a bedroom. Privacy was a luxury I could not afford there. Quickly I concluded it would be better to find a flatmate who was already paying for light and space. I could use the company — I knew only two people in the city of millions — and I could always move.

After that first week, I would be on my own. But the prospect of attending theatre off-off-Broadway, kicking around my favourite museums — the Frick, the Metropolitan — and occasionally warming a bar stool at one of the less tourist-riddled jazz clubs, was thrilling. Surely I would meet some interesting people at the playwrights' course for which I had registered. I had even packed my tennis racquet, recently dusted off after years of disuse, in the hope I would meet others for whom running was pointless unless it was in pursuit of a ball.

I did not worry about the bigger questions, such as where I would live, or how quickly I would find work (my goal was to use my communications and grant-making experience in the enormous US philanthropic sector). I had nothing to fear, because I had nothing to lose. Looming larger as I prepared to depart Sydney were questions relating to the smaller details of daily life: who would I trust to cut my hair, for example, or to wax my legs?

~

Later, after all the guests had left my farewell party, I wandered through the house by myself, as I had done countless times over the eighteen months since John died. Though emptied of most of its contents, its items packed carefully into labelled boxes, the place still felt like home to me. I wondered what I would miss the most when faced with having to set up a new home in New York. The light that streamed through the living room windows, or the photograph of the white bridge that hangs on one of its walls? My piano, or the view of the garden from the back deck? The spacious kitchen, or the fig tree where we exchanged our vows? A new door was opening, but the old doors had not closed. They were the same doors that had been in place for years; their wood had simply been treated and painted. I might be leaving the house, but I was not leaving John.

My efforts to sort through the detritus of our shared and individual lives — at first an unconscious process helping me to feel a sense, however misplaced, of order and control — evolved into a much more conscious series of choices about how I wanted my home to look, and how I wanted to live. Despite the time I spent flicking through magazines and catalogues, my home improvements sought an emotional, rather than a material, transformation. John and I had spent our life together in a state of constant change, but throughout it all we placed great value on the life we lived together in our home. I believe that my home now honours the life John and I made there, but it is *my* home now. My connection to it is as strong as it ever was, but the reasons for that connection are healthier than they were when I first set out to address the rising damp.

As the months passed, and my house slowly turned from sodden sponge to dried and aerated edifice, the broader parallels between home and self inevitably emerged. Now, looking back over my first year and a half as a young widow, I'm surprised it took me as long as it did to notice the extent of the metaphor. To connect the excessive damp in my house's foundations with the intense grief of losing John. While watching the contractors at work inside my house I could witness the problem of damp being addressed and remedied; their slow pace and care offered a parallel to the glacial, unpredictable and curling patterns that my own 'damp crisis' presented. Of the two forms of damp, my grief proved to be the more persistent, but there was no short cut I could find to fix it, no outsourcing its repair. The experience of grief, different though it must be for every bereaved person, is not a straight line. Straight lines are best left to geometry and theory.

The rest of my life will always be with John, and without him. His is a permanent absence that, like negative space, shapes my life. Sometimes it's difficult even for me to believe that the history of our private world — from beginning to end, and everything that happened in between — occurred in the space of two years. And that we experienced in that time tremendous joy and exhilaration, which we found and lost so much sooner than we wanted or imagined. My loss is like a bruise that is no longer visible on the surface of my skin, but remains tender to the touch.

I am alert to the power of transient moments, as fleeting as a chord change, the sight of a butterfly fluttering its wings, or the smile of a stranger. I can smile back, recognising that we are both human, alive, wanting connection to something greater than ourselves, with the terrible privilege of knowing that such connection, though rare, is possible.

It is time for me to take flight. Moving to New York is the next step in finding out what *a rich and full life* might look like, feel like. John is part of me now, his joy of living and his ambitions for my future in which he would never be directly on stage. Just constantly in the wings. My love for him and the fire of those brief years we spent together have inevitably forged a different version of me. But John does not define me. His death does not define me, either, but that event has altered my life in ways I never imagined.

I have travelled a long way inside this house. Now, with the rising damp fixed and the house painted and the garden pruned to within an inch of its life, I can look around me and *see* that it is the same house it has always been, transformed by time and love and renovation. An old house that is also a new house, an ending and a beginning.

Acknowledgements

I would like to thank University of Chicago Press for permission to quote Natalia Ginzburg's poem 'Memory' from Natalia Ginzburg, *It's Hard to Talk About Yourself*, edited by Cesare Garboli and Lisa Ginzburg, translated by Louise Quirke, © The University of Chicago 2003.

An earlier version of chapter 20 appeared in *Griffith Review* 17, 'Staying Alive'.

I am grateful to my parents, Pam and John, and to my brother, Trent, for their unfailing support before, during, and since the events described in these pages.

Although most of the book was written in solitude in a Brooklyn apartment, it would not have emerged without the support of these dear alphabetised friends: Lily Brett, Alex Carr, Sally Devenish, Susan Jerome, Simi Linton, John Moore, Cheryl Smith, Derek Van Gieson, Ton Wilson, Debra Workman.

Madonna Duffy encouraged me that there was a book in my early scribbles, and expertly helped me to find it. Thank you for your enthusiasm and insight.

For their feedback on subsequent drafts I am indebted to Madeleine Beckman, Jennifer Fleming, Margot Meyers, Snowdon Parlette, Kate Veitch, Ed Wright.

Thank you to University of Queensland Press for sharing my vision of this book, and to Alexandra Payne in particular for shepherding it with such professional care.

Finally, I would like to acknowledge Kathryn Lovric's help with the rising damp, but its value is beyond words.